Stress-Free
Home Downsizing

Stress-Free Home Downsizing

A **Senior's Guide**

to **Selling Your House**

and **Simplifying Your Life**

Ben Souchek

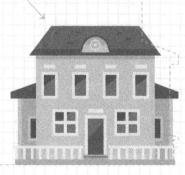

Advantage | Books

Published by Advantage Books, Charleston, South Carolina.
An imprint of Advantage Media.

ADVANTAGE is a registered trademark, and the Advantage colophon is a trademark of Advantage Media Group, Inc.

Printed in the United States of America.

10 9 8 7 6 5 4 3 2 1

ISBN: 978-1-64225-946-9 (Paperback)
ISBN: 978-1-64225-945-2 (eBook)

Library of Congress Control Number: 2024900714

Cover and layout design by Matthew Morse.

This publication is designed to provide accurate and authoritative information in regard to the subject matter covered. It is sold with the understanding that the publisher is not engaged in rendering legal, accounting, or other professional services. If legal advice or other expert assistance is required, the services of a competent professional person should be sought.

Advantage Books is an imprint of Advantage Media Group. Advantage Media helps busy entrepreneurs, CEOs, and leaders write and publish a book to grow their business and become the authority in their field. Advantage authors comprise an exclusive community of industry professionals, idea-makers, and thought leaders. For more information go to **advantagemedia.com**.

*This book is dedicated to all the professionals that help seniors
and their families make the downsizing transition
to a smaller home, apartment, or senior living community…*

And especially to the seniors and their families making the transition!

*May this book serve as a guide and companion
to provide an easier, stress-free path.*

Contents

PART I

Professionals Who Help with Moving Out

Introduction

I didn't know the real estate model was broken when I began twenty-five years ago. Didn't know that it worked much better for the agents than those selling their houses. But time after time, I'd speak with senior home sellers who were deeply frustrated with the whole process. They'd been told by agents that they had to clear away all their belongings. Been told they had to make these repairs and those upgrades and then a bunch more if they hoped to sell at a good price. But these seniors didn't want to jump through dozens of hoops. They just wanted to sell the house and move on.

Seeing all this happen time and again, I just figured there had to be a better way.

A better way for a senior to go through the whole downsizing process with dignity, ideally. But certainly with a lot less stress. And it was then that I began building that very thing. In time, my solution to the broken real estate model would become known as *Home Downsizing Solutions*. It would help seniors in the most immediate way: by turning this big life-changing transition from a drudgery into a delight—almost!

And today I'm sharing this service on a complimentary basis, opening it up to everybody. That includes introducing you to all the professionals who can make the downsizing experience a far more enjoyable and stress-free experience.

In these pages, you'll meet the men and women who can be trusted at each level of downsizing. All are here. Also here are the best practices to follow at each step in a downsizing, as well as the pitfalls to avoid. Both are important because a successful downsizing can really only be spoiled one way: by failing to do your homework and ending up with the wrong advisors, making the wrong moves.

Starting now, that won't have to happen.

I'll share the good and bad about the downsizing business. And in as few words as possible (keeping the reading short!) I'll hopefully help you make the right decisions for yourself or a loved one going forward.

It begins with a question: Is it even time to be downsizing? It's a good question because if it's not the right time, then there's no sense reading on! Or at least, not yet. Though sooner or later, a decision must be made by every senior together with a caring family.

☐ Is the current house still useful, or have the events that have taken place over the many years in the house changed the value of the house to the senior?

☐ Is it safe to remain in the house—that is, can the senior be taken care of properly there?

☐ Does a move to a smaller home or apartment or a retirement community make more sense now? Or, will it soon?

I aim to answer these questions by introducing you to the trusted professionals in your local area who can assist in your decision-making at each step along the path to this next chapter in life.

In Part I of the book, you'll meet the different professionals involved in the transition out of the current house. That begins with *Home Caregivers* who are often the first to know a senior's real needs. We'll talk about finding a caregiver you can trust, how to vet them properly for extra peace of mind, and what costs to expect along with the role insurance plays.

We'll turn next to *Senior Move Managers*, showing how to find the right help for a smoother and hassle-free move, planning out the moving day, dealing with all the "stuff" in the house, holding down the costs, and protecting against fraud or any mishaps along the way.

If the move will take you or a loved one to a retirement community, a *Senior Placement Agent* is the expert in selecting the community best suited to your current and future needs. We'll look at how to select the best agent in your area, along with the living options available to you and the costs to expect.

If in moving out there is a need for an estate sale or auction of property, there are a number of options for holding tasteful, successful estate sales. So we'll look at *Estate Sale/Auction Professionals* and help you decide which is the better choice for your family.

Having the right advice at this point in life is critical to ensuring that the senior's rights and assets are well-secured, and that the next generation is provided for in the manner desired. *Elder Care and Estate Attorneys* each play a role here, and we'll talk about how to select the attorney you can trust and then use their skill sets to your fullest advantage.

In Part II, you'll learn about the professionals who play a role in the move to a senior living community, beginning with *Senior Community Managers*. You'll meet the community's two key players—the Executive Manager and the Marketing Manager. And you'll see how to tour a senior community to learn everything you need to feel confident that you are choosing the right community.

Next are the *Medical Social Workers*, the everyday angels working in hospitals and helping families through difficult times. We'll talk about the duties and extra care these individuals provide, and how they can make sure the hospital's Discharge Plan truly serves the patient upon release back to the home or next step in life.

A similar role is played by *Hospital Ombuds*—advocates for a patient in the hospital and upon leaving. Often called in to resolve a problem over medical care, the Ombud can also help ensure that the patient's next steps after the hospital are the right ones.

From here we move on to *Paying for the Care You Deserve*, including applying for and getting government assistance, taking out the right insurance policy, grabbing tax breaks you're owed, falling back on a reverse mortgage if necessary, lowering the costs of assisted living, selling the house at the right time, and even selling the house but being allowed to remain living in it (a wonderful option!).

Finally in Part III, we'll look at the real estate portion of downsizing and show you how we're *Turning Downsizing into a Delight (Almost!)*. You'll see how to go about downsizing the right way so that your stuff all finds the right new home, your house is prepped to sell, you enjoy a smooth move out with a successful closing, and you're onto the new home that's best for you.

We'll then take a step back with *A Reality Check before Selling the House* and make sure you don't fall into any traps or take any wrong turns. There are important things to get right in preparing the house for sale, putting it on the market, dealing with the ups and downs of showings, and potential closing cost surprises you want to avoid.

There are *Options for Selling a House*, and we'll look at the pros and cons of each as they relate to your situation, to your needs. There's the traditional real estate agent, selling the house yourself, or working with a home buying company.

Lastly we'll focus on *Finding the Right Real Estate Professional* by giving you the questions to ask any professional at each stage of the process. In this way, you'll have confidence that your house sale and move into a new living arrangement will deliver all the comfort and care you or a loved one deserves.

Either a handful or all of these professionals could become part of your own custom downsizing solution. It's a solution available to you through our *Home Downsizing Solutions Network* that's expanding nationwide.

Indeed, as part of this expansion, we are looking to identify downsizing professionals who are standout performers in their communities. We want to recognize these standouts with *Downsizing Triumph of the Year* awards for all their efforts in providing this important service to seniors in our communities.

If you work with professionals you believe are qualified for this award, we encourage you to contact us and nominate them for consideration. You can do this in a number of ways.

- *Call our office*: 855-291-5005
- *Visit our website*: HomeDownsizingSolutions.com
- *Scan this QR code* with your phone and begin a text conversation with our team

Now let's move ahead with a look at the professionals who could become important advisors and partners with your family in the years ahead.

1

Is It Time to Begin Downsizing?

HIGHLIGHTS

▶ Are recent changes in your life affecting your living situation?

▶ What is "staying put" in your house going to look like?

▶ Might a move make sense financially?

▶ Who can best help with your next move?

"Honey!" MaryAnne shouted in that voice which meant "please come now."

But Herb didn't reply, not even after several attempts. And they'd just checked Herb's hearing. It hadn't deteriorated that much.

Getting a little worried, MaryAnne went searching for her husband of thirty-eight years. And found him in the laundry room, wedged back behind too many cardboard boxes stacked high with the kids' old skiing equipment and books Herb refused to part with and all the silver tableware they'd long ago inherited but never used.

Herb's arms were buried deep into the back of the dryer, and he was cursing it more than fixing it, from the look of things. That's when MaryAnne realized three things one after another.

One, Herb hadn't even heard her on the other side of a house that had a lot more square footage than they needed now that the kids were launched into their own lives.

Two, the old house was starting to need repairs that Herb just shouldn't be doing anymore.

And three, they hadn't really gotten out of that old house much in recent years. Hadn't gone out to the street since their longtime neighbor friends had moved away. Hadn't traveled much either—and that's what had always nourished their marriage.

With that came a fourth realization, a question really, which she put to Herb, "This is our last big journey in life, honey; what should it look like for us?"[1]

Maybe you're having similar thoughts about how your life has changed since you first moved into your house. If you've been wondering if that house is still the best fit for you today, well, you're in good company.

Two out of three seniors end up moving to a new location at least once in their retirement years, with about five million taking the next step this year.[2]

As numbers go, 83 percent of them are remaining in their same state. As for those moving further, the favorite destinations are the South Atlantic, the mountain states, and the Pacific coast in that order.[3]

Reasons for moving?

Number one is to be closer to family, followed by a desire to cut down on home expenses, a need to deal with health issues, and lastly a change in marital status.

But how might it look for you? As we enter our sixties, we approach and begin to cross what's known as the "freedom threshold"—and what a threshold it is!

On the other side of this threshold is our next chapter in life. Crossing over may not result in any eye-popping changes in our life, not at first anyway. Many of us choose to stay in our houses as long as possible. Only when necessary will we want to downsize into a smaller house, or an apartment or condo, or some kind of senior living community.

So when will it become necessary? Perhaps when you find yourself having the conversations I hear often. Conversations about having too much stuff:

With the kids gone I thought we'd have an extra room we could use for exercise or our new hobby. But it seems to have become a large closet for all our accumulated stuff! And what a lot of stuff! And a lot of conflicted feelings to go with it. We know logically that we don't need to keep all these possessions, yet our hearts tell us otherwise. For this is the stuff of our life, with so many memories. How could we ever throw it out?

Conversations about talking in circles:

We have this classic circular conversation. You know, the one where we get all excited and start planning a home remodel, and think about making it just right, only then realizing how expensive it will be, and how that money must come out of the "for living" fund. And the conversation stalls out until it comes up again, and we run the circle again.

Conversations about living in a two-story house:

Sadly, we had a health event and the old house just doesn't work in its current form. Some other living arrangement has to be worked out, and probably soon. But frankly, the thought of dealing with any of this is just overwhelming.

Conversations like these are clues to the direction our lives are taking. But only clues. For me, it helps to get a little more concrete. To ask some specific questions that can open the eyes to what's coming. Specific questions include the following:

- ☐ Has climbing stairs become a challenge?
- ☐ Is it tough to access higher cabinets and storage spaces?
- ☐ Is installing grab bars and safety devices becoming necessary?
- ☐ Can the windows be kept clean, or is that no longer possible?
- ☐ Have the garden and landscaping been ignored lately?
- ☐ Is there a steep driveway that creates a risk of falling?
- ☐ Is mowing the lawn, or shoveling snow, becoming difficult?

A bunch of "yes" answers tells us that at the very least, a smaller single-level home may be a smart choice in the near future.

It turns out that nearly half of seniors, even if fully healthy, have a hard time navigating stairs.[4] And the National Council on Aging tells us that one in four of us over age sixty-five will fall this year.[5]

These are the kinds of "statistics" we'd rather just ignore because they can weigh heavily on us and stress us out. We can find ourselves paralyzed into inaction, putting off decisions until it's too late to make good ones.

So that that doesn't happen, let's walk through the choices we have ahead.

Are recent changes in your life affecting your living situation?

They say that change is the only constant, and surely it's true. But it's also true that when we've been in a house for a while—years turning into decades—that we think less in terms of change than constancy. The constancy of a house that has been there through the ups and downs of our journey through life.

After a while, we find that we are in a house for different reasons than when we began.

Think about it. How much of the house do you really use now? Is there a room or two that rarely gets used, except to store things, or for guests or when the kids visit? Is all the yardwork and those weekend visits to Lowe's for the latest repair still something you enjoy, or at least tolerate? Or could that burden be offloaded, thank you very much?

Perhaps you've been in your house long enough to notice that favorite neighborhood friends have moved away or passed on. For some of us, this can trigger actual feelings of loneliness, even if the younger families moving in bring new life to the street.

We often have more time on our hands as we approach retirement, and we wonder what else is out there, or how would it feel to indulge a long-held wanderlust and just hop into an RV and see where the road leads, or explore living in another environment, or take some classes, or pick up a new hobby for a new lease on life, as they say.

And in thinking about this, we get a better idea of how our current house is working for us. Quite possibly, it's working just swell, and that's good. But then again, it might not be. A house that once fit your lifestyle like a glove might be tattered and torn now. And like that old glove, you may be feeling torn over the idea of downsizing.

It can feel like a charged topic—because it is!

It can also be flipped into a freeing topic if approached like a walk across the "freedom threshold" into a new way of living.

Is there freedom in a simpler life?

For some, this will feel like a loaded question. Answer in the affirmative, and it suggests a certain lack of ambition. Or in the negative, a kind of James Dean recklessness!

But truly, it is natural and healthy to seek a more stress-free environment as we age. "To sit under my own vine and fig tree … in peaceful retirement," as George Washington wrote upon leaving public life.

After dedicating an adult life to joyful responsibilities—to a career, to raising a family—now there's a new threshold. Crossing over to the things you want to be doing because they appeal, not simply because you've been doing them for so long.

Anyone who owns a house knows how much time and effort are gobbled up simply in maintaining it. And how much stuff stacks up to fill the available space over the years, often flowing out of the house into storage units, taking on a life of its own.

The more possessions we have, the more hold they have on us. That can be comforting and limiting at the same time.

So what happens if you let go? If you turn down the energy you spend on the large house and all the possessions? Or at least the ones that don't pass what I call

The 365 Test:
I haven't seen or used
[NAME A POSSESSION]
for over a year!

How would life change if these possessions were given a new home, where they are again useful? Who could benefit? As for you, there would be less cleaning and upkeep, that's for sure.

In a way, downsizing can turn into an upsizing. Moving into a smaller home with fewer possessions and obligations can launch a new frame of mind. Call it an upsized mind because it allows a clearer, crisper understanding of what's most important in this new chapter of life.

A life of fewer obligations.

Fewer obligations to the property itself. To the extra bedrooms, or the home office, or the game room and big garage and all the rest. Rooms that may no longer be getting any use but, if kept, still require cleaning, heating or cooling, insurance coverage, and taxes paid on their portion of the whole.

Fewer obligations to update the decor. Sure, it can be fun to choose wall coverings, carpet colors, and window treatments for all the rooms. But as much fun as it once was?

Fewer obligations to maintenance. All the minor repairs, the painting, the mowing the lawn, the wintertime joy of shoveling snow are nobody's idea of a relaxing weekend. And sooner or later, these projects do become a physical challenge.

Interestingly, selling the house while it's still in good condition can save the need for many of those big repair and maintenance expenses. Selling the house at the right time can net you considerable money, in fact.

But first...

What is "staying put" in your house going to look like?

"What is one million houses?" is the Jeopardy answer to, "The number of houses in America set up for aging in place." There are about a hundred million houses in America, but only one in a hundred is ready for an aging occupant. That doesn't matter, of course, until a health issue presents itself. Then the modifications and upgrades begin.

There's no shortage of home construction companies willing to help. As well, the National Association of Home Builders (nahb.com) offers a directory of contractors trained in designing and building good-looking, aging-in-place environments.

For an idea of the costs of modifying your current house, look at this chart. It shows the most common projects on the remodeling checklist:

Costs of Remodeling Your House to Age in Place

Prices vary by location.

PROJECT	PRICE RANGE	AVG. PRICE
Widen Hallways	$20,000 to $40,000	$32,000
Remodel Kitchen & Appliances	$15,000 to $27,000	$19,000
Install a Stair Lift	$3,500 to $21,000	$9,000
Install a Walk-in Tub or Shower	$3,000 to $18,000	$7,000
Widen an Entry Door	$400 to $6,500	$2,000
Install Hand and Guard Rails	$700 to $5,200	$3,000
Install Ramp at Entrance	$800 to $2,200	$1,000
TOTAL	**$43,400 TO $120,100**	**$73,000**

So for the average house, the remodel bill can run to $73,000. And while most of us won't need all these fixes, deciding what to remodel is made difficult by all the unknowns. Will mobility become an issue? Will a wheelchair be needed? Could an elevator be called for (not even included in the above costs)? It's just hard to know.

Fortunately, you can get help in identifying medically required house modifications if you have Medicare Part B. They'll pay an Occupational Therapist to come in and assess what's needed. And then, if you have Medicare Part C supplemental insurance, you may be able to get some of the modifications paid for.

Another way to pay for these expenses is a reverse mortgage. This is a way for homeowners sixty-two and older to borrow money using the home as security for the loan. Funds from the reverse mortgage can be used to pay for everyday bills, to repair or modify a home, or to pay for long-term care when needed.

The downside of this approach is the obvious one—the home is not an unlimited piggybank, and it's very easy to run out of money before you run out of life. And with inflation returning to levels not seen in decades, the costs of living can quickly eat through this home store of cash.

This becomes more apparent when seniors begin to need day-to-day assistance.

Bringing a caregiver into the house can be a lifesaver after an injury, or when the eyesight goes and driving is no longer an option. But caregivers earn between $20 and $50 an hour—depending on the experience they bring and your location. This is a manageable fee for a valuable service. But as the need for caregiving moves from part-time to full-time, the costs can become steep. Then the aging-in-place option will usually have to be reevaluated on a cost-benefit basis. At that point, moving to a smaller home frees up cash to pay for needed caregiving.

Might a move make sense financially?

A typical home sold in America has recently dropped in size to 1,720 square feet, according to Redfin realtors.[6] This tells us that smaller homes are becoming more popular with people of all ages. There are other reasons, as well. Home prices have risen so dramatically that people have to choose smaller. And when interest rates are rising, it limits the size of the home people can afford. These facts have led some analysts to caution that moving to a smaller home won't produce the same cash savings as in years gone by.

But it's wise to look below the headlines, as it were.

The financial analysts and real estate gurus you see on TV news shows, and even in the newspaper and online, are usually affiliated with big-name real estate houses. They have a vested interest in your buying the priciest house you can possibly qualify for—even if that requires a Liar Loan (documents, who needs 'em?) or a Ninja Loan (No INcome, no Job, and no Assets). So they advise waiting for the markets to "cool off."

But how many years will it take for things to cool off? Nobody knows the future, even though the clock is ticking for all of us.

As for home prices, they have shot up. But—and this is a big but—prices have shot up for *all* homes over the past twenty years. For both middle- and lower-tier homes,[7] look at this chart:

U.S. Home Prices: 2003-2022

Source: National Association of Realtors

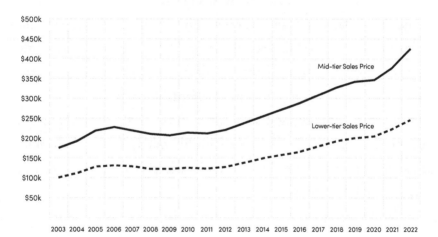

Notice how prices for mid-tier homes (basically the median price for a home in America) have gone from $178,900 to $428,700 in this two-decade span. At the same time, prices for lower-tier homes (smaller homes) have gone from $102,600 to $248,200. So the spread between the larger homes and the smaller homes has remained fairly steady.

Smaller homes are running about 57–59 percent less in price. If anything, the spread has widened a little in the last few years. So a move to a smaller home at this time would generate pretty much the same cash-in-hand as it used to.

Here's an illustration of that. Let's say you go ahead and move into a home that costs $100,000 less than your existing home. You could then be pocketing about $3,000 in income and $3,250 in housing costs each year. In five years, you would have an extra $31,250 in your pocket for other expenses, including the costs of aging that we've talked about.

That extra cash could become doubly important if you happen to experience a sudden drop in income from retiring or a job loss or salary cut. You'll need that cash to steer clear of the so-called trouble zone. That's the zone where your monthly rent or a mortgage payment rises higher than 30 percent of your monthly budget, leaving too little for other expenses. If that happens, it's the surest sign that it's time to look to a smaller home with a more affordable mortgage.

Moving into the right-sized home can drop that housing spend down to 15–20 percent of your monthly outlay, leaving you more financially stable, more able to handle unexpected expenses as they arise, overall less stressed and happier.

Which brings us to the final question …

Who can best help with your next move?

A move as important as downsizing is best done with all the expert assistance you can muster, relying on the experiences and insights of people who've been there. You want professionals in your corner who keep you fully informed of the whole picture, so you make the best decision for yourself.

That's why I've brought together all these experts in the pages to follow!

You'll meet people who specialize in the downsizing journey. People with experience in navigating around tricky or confusing obstacles in a short period of time, always keeping your personal goals front of mind. People such as the following:

- *Caregivers* who come into the house when health issues escalate and more intensive care is needed.

- *Senior Move Managers* who step in when it's time and help with each step of the move from one house to the other.

- *Estate Specialists* who come in and help sell or auction off the contents in a house, netting you the most proceeds in the shortest period of time.

- *Senior Placement Agents* who help decide if a family member needs to transition to another level of care because they can no longer be taken care of properly in the house. And then offer help in choosing the best senior living community for you.

- *Senior Community Managers* who handle marketing and management of their communities from the very first greeting and tour of the facilities through to ensuring that the care is provided as promised.

- *Social Workers* who offer a number of valuable services such as arranging for funds to pay for a senior community when finances are tight.

- *Hospital Ombuds* who can help when a senior no longer qualifies to stay in the hospital and needs to transition to another level of care.

- *Elder Law and Estate Attorneys* who handle all the legal aspects of downsizing and estates, including paying for care in a community.

And once you learn about the roles these professionals play, we'll continue on with the downsizing options available to you.

A SMALLER HOME

Moving into a smaller home to provide a home-like environment but without the burdens of a larger home.

A CONDO OR APARTMENT

If not much space is needed going forward, a condo or apartment still provides your own living space. Plus you can be in a complex with others in your age group if you desire such a social arrangement.

ADULT CHILD'S HOME

Moving in with the kids can be great—if all parties agree, of course! Sharing in a child's and grandchild's life is an obvious treasure in later years. It is not for everyone, but it is an option.

WHAT YOU NEED TO KNOW ABOUT RETIREMENT HOMES

If you or a loved one might be best situated in a living community in the next few years, begin making decisions now. Most communities have waiting lists—sometimes years-long waiting lists. Be sure to plan ahead.

AN INDEPENDENT LIVING COMMUNITY

Here you live in your own home or apartment within a shared complex that's designed for an independent and active lifestyle with recreational, social, and educational activities with your peers.

AN ASSISTED LIVING FACILITY

Here there's a higher level of supervision than independent living communities but not as intensive as a nursing home. Usually this is apartment-style living with services that include cooking, bathing, laundry, transportation, help with medications, and limited nursing help.

A SKILLED NURSING FACILITY

When twenty-four-hour care becomes needed, this is the option. Residents have a private room or share a room, depending on financial and health factors. All needed services, including medical and rehab therapies, are provided.

A CONTINUING CARE RETIREMENT COMMUNITY

Most flexible of all, these communities provide a range of options as needed by residents from independent living to assisted living to skilled nursing and long-term care facilities—all on the same property.

Those are the seven most popular living options—in addition to staying put, of course! It's a lot to think about. We'll look into the pros and cons of each one in the coming chapters. We'll meet the professionals who can help in this most important next step.

Is now the right time?

Leaving a house you've lived in for years is an emotional prospect. There's no way around it. That's why I put this book together, to give you a clear-headed ally in the decisions ahead. In this way you can put your best foot forward.

You can know if you should logically sell the house and downsize in order to enjoy life more or remain in place in a way that allows you to enjoy the life you have.

This book is also, of course, for adult children who want to make the best decision together with parents before those important decisions are thrust upon you by the passing years.

It's never easy to make a big change. Just know that help is in hand, literally! And as with any destination you set out for, the first step is to, well, take the first step.

And that begins with a plan.

You want to get clear on where you might go before selling your house, and then you can strategize the details of the move. Step 1 in this plan is to give yourself a timeline with goals and steps to reach them.

It can take six months and even longer to downsize, since there's plenty to do. But a six-month plan is a good start, and we have included one for you in the Worksheets at the end. For now, let's push ahead and figure out what belongs in your plan.

THE HOME DOWNSIZING SIX-MONTH PLAN

When ready to fill in your plan, you'll find a Worksheet to help in chapter 15 on page 177.

PART I

Professionals
Who Help with
Moving Out

2

Home Caregivers

HIGHLIGHTS

▶ Finding a caregiver you can trust
▶ Vetting your caregiver
▶ Knowing the costs and what's covered

It was a day Adele and Harry would never forget. It began with Adele insisting she'd never leave their old house and then ending in tears with Adele feeling horrible for all the pain she'd unknowingly caused Harry. And it happened on the eve of their golden wedding anniversary celebration, which now might not happen.

Adele's health had worsened that past year, with her diabetes leaving her exhausted, too tired to eat, catching one infection after another. But Harry had been there for her every step of the way, cutting back on his hospital job and his volunteer work at the Boy's Club.

At one point, Adele had insisted on bringing in an outside agency to help. But the results had been mixed. First a bad apple, but then a "doll of a lifesaver" as Harry had put it. But Harry had also done the math, and they couldn't afford outside care on their limited pensions.

So Harry had stepped up. His health had always been good, and he knew he could handle it. "Til death do us part," he'd always say. And when Adele, now forced to use a walker to inch into the kitchen that night to see what Harry was cooking, or burning from the smell of it, she found him face down on the floor.

Without hesitation, Adele pushed the medic alert button Harry had insisted she always wear. And a crackerjack response team had Harry to the hospital in no time. He was going to pull through. But, the doctor said, his heart attack was probably stress related, self-neglect related. All his strength was no match for the stress of caring nearly full-time for his wife.

Adele knew right then that their golden anniversary would only happen if they found a way to care for each other.

Caregiving gets so little attention in our society, and it's a terrible shame. It's so important to millions of older adults who can no longer feel "independent" in their current house without the help of caregivers.

Most of these caregivers are women caring for a loved one, giving around twenty hours a week of care and not being paid for it. This has raised a genuine public health concern because it can lead to physical, emotional, psychological, and financial strains.

One in four caregivers say the work had worsened their own health, according to an American Association of Retired Persons'

(AARP) study.[8] Two in ten caregivers say they had to quit their own jobs, and four in ten had to reduce their working hours to care for a loved one.[9]

Just the out-of-pocket expenses for caregiving can run from $7,000 to $9,000 a year, so the financial burden on top of the physical and emotional burden has created a difficult situation.

For most of us, the solutions to these problems follow a similar path. We try to take care of our loved ones for as long as feasible, then we bring in outside caregivers for as long as financially advisable, and then we look to move into the best independent or assisted living arrangement we can afford.

Let's look at that progression.

Caregivers can enrich the life of a senior

Usually seniors are happiest and healthiest where they are most comfortable—in their current house. They want to remain in place as long as feasible. So when the time comes to bring in caregivers, it gives everyone peace of mind to know that compassionate and skilled professionals are on the job.

From part-time care and companionship to around-the-clock monitoring, a caregiver or caregiving team can offer a range of services so that a senior can confidently age in place in the familiarity and comfort of the current house.

A good caregiver will have four responsibilities:

- *Personal assistance.* Giving help as needed with bathing and dressing, housekeeping, errands, and transportation services.
- *Healthy nutrition.* Providing a nutritious and balanced diet is essential and often neglected by seniors. Going out shopping

for healthy food and preparing it for the senior can be a big part of a good day.

- *Wellness monitoring.* It gets difficult for seniors to keep the schedules they once handled easily. Regular monitoring becomes essential. Reminders to eat, drink, and take meds on schedule. In-home monitoring technologies can help, as well, when the caregiver is busy or away. Medical alert systems provide peace of mind for the families who may live far away.
- *Kind companionship.* One of the hardest parts of aging is the loneliness that comes, naturally, as the family has moved away and friends begin passing away. So it's important for caregivers to keep a senior mentally engaged in conversation as well as taking regular outings to help with their mental health.

Finding a caregiver you can trust

There are two types of caregivers who come into the home:

☐ *Health aides* who supervise basic medical care, such as managing medication and checking blood pressure. They can be the right choice if a senior has an illness or a disability and requires trained medical attention.

☐ *Personal care aides* who help with bathing, eating, dressing, household chores, preparing meals, scheduling activities, and offering companionship during the day.

Many caregivers can provide both services, so deciding which one is needed, or if both are needed, is Step 1 in interviewing for help.

Step 2, though I've found it often occurs first, is preparing your loved one for a stranger coming into their house. Many seniors refuse to admit they need help for fear of losing their independence, understandably. So it's important for everyone involved to ease into this. Begin with baby steps. Perhaps hire a caregiver for a single task—doing the cooking or laundry. This easing-in process can help in more than one way, actually.

Fact is, it can turn into a stressful, time-consuming project to find and then manage outside help. You need to find someone who is trustworthy, with the right skill sets, whom you are comfortable with. You might not find this caregiver or a team of two to three caregivers to cover all your needs, until you have "tried out" a couple of them. So starting someone on a part-time basis makes it easier and less expensive to ensure that they are a good fit.

Most people begin searching for caregivers by asking family and friends, a doctor or a local support organization. This kind of word of mouth can be a good way to find an independent caregiver or a home health agency recommendation.

There are thousands of agencies specializing in home care. To find one in your area, you can turn to any of the following:

- Eldercare Locator, a free service of
  the U.S. Administration on Aging:
    - 1-800-677-1116
    - eldercare.acl.gov/Public/Index.aspx

- The National Association for Home Care & Hospice:
    - https://agencylocator.nahc.org

There are several directories of independent caregivers where you can gather a group of candidates based on your preferred criteria and then contact and interview them.

Some of these directories, such as Care.com, will do background checks on your candidates for an extra fee.

Early on, you want to decide whether to hire a caregiver through an agency or on your own. There are pros and cons to each:

AGENCY	
Pros	**Cons**
They do background screenings and are licensed and bonded to protect against theft or abuse	You have less choice in who comes to your home
They do the hiring and firing	They often divide the job between several workers, so it's difficult to develop a deep relationship
They do the tax and legal paperwork	Cost is usually higher
YOU HIRE	
Pros	**Cons**
You select the person you like most	You handle interviews, schedules, duties, payroll, and taxes
Cost is usually lower	If the caregiver is sick, you arrange backup

Vetting your caregiver

As we all know, there are scam artists in all walks of life, including home healthcare. Caregivers come into the homes of seniors who usually have more wealth than the caregiver does. And the senior is often less attentive to the goings-on around them than they once were. This opens the door to caregiver wrongdoing that all but the most honest cannot resist. And so seniors can be bilked out of their wealth with forged checks, stolen jewelry, or sold-off valuables.

Some simple steps can be taken to ensure that a caregiver is held accountable and the senior is not taken advantage of.

The key is to basically firewall all financial accounts and valuables. Put in place a "low ceiling" on the credit cards and bank account, along with alerts. These accounts can always be replenished so that a senior does not feel that their independence is being taken away but that safeguards are in place.

If you're hiring an independent caregiver without an agency, do a background check. Ask for references from former employers, and be sure to call them. Use a service to check criminal histories and driving records. Also call to verify that the license is current for anyone who is licensed.

When interviewing caregivers, be sure to ask probing questions about how they've handled difficult situations or disputes with their charges in the past. This can reveal a lot about their skills and their character.

And make sure the senior is part of the interview and selection process. Often it's wise for the adult children to pre-interview a handful of candidates and then have the senior meet and do their own interviews with the finalists. This can make the process easier for everyone.

When the caregiver begins to work in the house, it's best if a family member or friend is there during the first few days to make sure all goes smoothly.

Also, set up regular times for the adult children to talk to the caregiver by phone, to ensure that everyone is on the same page and happy with each other.

Know the costs and what's covered

Caregivers can charge between $20 and $50 an hour for typically a forty-four-hour work week, which equates to between $44,000 and $110,000 a year for full-time care.[10] If you'll also need help on weekends, evenings, or holidays, the prices rise accordingly.

Obviously, these costs can add up fast and can drain the finances of many families, which is why it's important to think it through. Will there be enough cash to cover expenses for the years ahead? And if not, are there better options than in-home caregiving? We'll talk more about these options as we proceed.

Many people are surprised to find that Medicare doesn't cover long-term care needs of any kind. But Medicare does pay for some short-term needs, such as after a person has been hospitalized or has an illness and a doctor certifies the need for specific care at home. We'll talk more about paying for care in chapter 10.

For now, on the financial front, keep in mind that there are rules about hiring caregivers. For instance, if you hire a family member or a friend as a caregiver and you pay them in cash under the table, you could get in trouble with the Internal Revenue Service (IRS). You need to be able to prove that the money you've paid wasn't a gift, which is a big deal for Medicaid eligibility later. Medicaid has what they call "spend down" rules that can disqualify a senior from receiving Medicaid funding for assisted living that may later be needed. Again, we'll talk more about this later.

If you pay caregivers either $2,000 or more in a year's period or $1,000 or more in a single quarterly period, you'll need to give them a W-2 form. A certified public accountant (CPA) can help with this, as can QuickBooks Payroll or a similar software product designed for a home-based care situation.

You should also check the individual's immigration status as their official employer.

If a caregiver is injured in your home and sues, you should know that your homeowner's insurance may not cover all the medical or legal costs. The resulting liability could be devastating, so it needs to be considered, no matter the likelihood. Check with your insurance agent about purchasing umbrella liability coverage. In some states, you might also need to purchase workers' compensation and disability benefits insurance.

All of these suggest that there are plenty of pluses and minuses to bringing a caregiver into the house. As well, as we saw in the opening story of this chapter, there are also concerns about a spouse becoming the caregiver. This can become a very difficult situation if not well managed. Providing support for the caregiver is sometimes just as important as the caregiver's work itself. It's good to check in on caregivers regularly to make sure they're managing their own health needs.

And when it comes time to move out of the home, whenever that may be, the goal will be to make the move as effortlessly as possible onto the next chapter in life. And that's why we'll talk next about Senior Move Managers.

Senior Move Managers

"I can't help you with the entire move, Mom," Phillip told his eighty-six-year-old mother, Josie. "But I've got it worked out for you; please don't worry!"

"Not worry? How can I . . .," Josie trailed off. She knew this would be her last move, and the whole process looked so dark. All the moving people coming into the house she'd long shared with her husband now passed. Picking up and moving to a new state, a new house, and not knowing anyone in the new location. How could her son possibly understand what she was going through?

"Mom, I know you're thinking only the worst, but there's also a lot of good that will come from moving."

"I know I have to move at my age, but ..."

"Mom, there are people who can step in and help you through it all . . . in the way you want . . . so you should have no worries about the movers mishandling your things or any of that."

"I don't know, dear ..."

"These people, Mom, they are called Senior Move Managers. They just handle it all. So let me arrange an interview with a couple of them, and you choose the one you like. OK, Mom?"

Oh yes, a move can be an overwhelming experience. No matter someone's age, it's just a lot. That's why Senior Move Managers have become so popular—they handle all aspects of the move, from the littlest worry to the largest, depending on your needs. Here's a look at the services they can provide.

How a Senior Move Manager can customize the move to your needs

A WORKSHEET

Preparing

- ☐ Talk to you about your general hopes and expectations for this move.
- ☐ Based on this input, create a timeline and checklists of tasks to do.
- ☐ Draw up a floor plan for where furnishings will go in the new home.
- ☐ Help find and engage a moving company and set a move date.

❏ Inventory the house and help decide what to take, sell, or give away.

❏ Pack and label items to move.

Moving

❏ Oversee the careful and efficient packing of items to move.

❏ At the new home, help unpack and prepare the new space.

❏ Position the furniture and art in the new space.

❏ Connect electronics, appliances, and computers.

❏ Dispose of packing materials.

Add-ons (as desired)

❏ Hold an estate sale for unwanted items.

❏ Arrange for unmoved items to be sold or donated.

❏ Arrange to clean and repair the old house in preparation for sale.

Finding the right Senior Move Manager for you

To select a Senior Move Manager you can trust, a smart approach is to begin with the nationwide group that accredits professionals in your state: the National Association of Senior Move Managers (NASMM). Find their listings at nasmm.org/find-a-move-manager.

Your state may have a lot of listings, so be sure to (a) use the zip code search tool to find professionals near you and (b) review all the listings before narrowing down and choosing two to three to interview in person.

All NASMM-accredited professionals have completed a twenty-five-hour training program in the essential skills and tools needed to run a safe and ethical practice, and they are screened for insurance. Still, confirm that the professional you hire is currently insured.

Another source for professional help is the National Association of Productivity & Organizing Professionals. They handle a number of organizing and productivity projects, as the name suggests. And one of those is downsizing management. Find their listings at pro.napo.net.

Generally, a Senior Move Manager won't be the one doing the heavy lifting. They will help as needed at every step, and having them there to oversee the actual loading of the truck will be a comforting feeling.

Planning for a smooth move day

At least four to six months before your actual moving date, if possible, begin working with your Senior Move Manager on the first steps. There is plenty to get done.

Your move manager will not be doing the actual moving, of course, but can help you in selecting a professional moving company that is capable and trustworthy.

Using a professional mover makes a lot of sense, because they can handle a move in less time and even less cost than hiring people yourself. They know the ins and outs of the process and can do everything quicker and more efficiently. And they are going to be more trustworthy—a key thing, as we'll discuss. Whether the move will take you across town or across the country, a professional moving company makes sense.

If you have a choice of when to move, consider moving in the "off-season." That means anytime but summer. "High season" for moving companies is in the summer months, and their availability is likely to be tighter, harder to schedule.

Whichever time window you choose, be sure to do it as far in advance as possible so that you can reserve and lock in the services of a reputable mover and avoid scheduling conflicts.

You can also usually save money by moving in the off-season or during the middle of the month, when movers are less busy.

Organizing ahead of time

If you need a change of address with the Postal Service, you can go to usps.com and do that. It's the ideal method, and USPS will send you an email confirmation right away. You can also ask USPS to temporarily change your address at:

- usps.com/manage/forward.htm

Or to hold your mail:

- holdmail.usps.com/holdmail

You will also need to contact a few government agencies with your change of address. They want to keep up with you, of course! You may need to file forms at the IRS, Social Security, Veterans Affairs, your state Department of Motor Vehicles (DMV), and election offices.

Be sure to tend to your financial accounts, including banks, credit cards, and insurance. Also, update any organizations you belong to or professionals you work with, such as lawyers, accountants, and doctors.

Make a list of the utilities at your old house to discontinue service. Set a date for a few weeks after you move to cancel services such as electric, gas, propane, water, heating oil, sewer, cable, internet, telephone, trash, and recycling. (You want some wiggle room in case of a delay in the move!)

You may also have an alarm system, sprinkler, pest control, newspaper delivery, or food service deliveries that need to be shut off.

Take pictures of all your belongings and the layout of each room. It will help when it comes time for the actual move and set-up of your new home. Taking pictures of the back of your TV and computer will help the people setting up your new home do it faster.

Get going on the easy, light packing even before bringing in a Senior Move Manager. It's good to start early with this because packing away your most sentimental items can unleash a flood of emotions. Give yourself time to reflect on the memories as they come bubbling back to the surface. This can be a good time, for these are the memories of this house that you'll take with you.

Be sure to pack valuables such as expensive jewelry and important documents in a carrier you personally take with you to your new home.

Holding down the costs of moving

If you hire a Senior Move Manager, expect to pay between $40 and $80 an hour for their services. So a total fee can run between $500 and $1,500, depending on how involved the Senior Move Manager gets.

Then there are the movers. Their prices are regulated, and you can ask to see those fees. Moves are usually billed using a weight/volume equation or by the amount of time the move takes. That's why you'll usually be given a nonbinding estimate, with the total price determined after the move. You can request a fixed price estimate, known as a binding estimate, but if you do, expect it to be higher. Note that if you cannot make payment on delivery, your possessions may be held in a warehouse.

Actual moving costs, according to Rocket Mortgage, will run in this range.[11]

TYPE OF MOVE	LOW END	HIGH END
Under 100 miles	$900	$2,500
Over 100 miles	$3,000	$10,000

Obviously, more complicated moves such as those involving an auto, piano, or animal pens, as well as a longer move such as coast to coast, can cost more. But these are good averages for planning purposes.

Protecting against fraud and mishap

With thirty-five million Americans moving every year, and the process being stressful under the best of circumstances, it makes sense to have a Senior Move Manager lighting the way. Even then, it's a good idea to double-check that the actual moving company you hire is trustworthy.

All too often a scam operator will win a moving contract by offering a lowball estimate. But after the work begins, they hold the belongings hostage until you pay thousands of dollars more. There are five ways to protect against this happening:

1. GET RECOMMENDATIONS

Be careful about relying on newspaper, phone book, or online ads for movers. Better to get recommendations from friends and family, reliable real estate agents, or, ideally, a Senior Move Manager. Plan to obtain estimates from at least three companies.

Avoid movers that don't provide a recognizable address or licensing information. Look at their trucks. Is the company name and logo printed on the side panels, as it should be, or are the truck panels blank—a sign of a fly-by-night outfit? In addition, never hire a mover who gives you an estimate over the phone or email or one requiring a large deposit.

A reputable company will send a representative to walk through your house properly and provide an accurate quote. This process is also an excellent way to collect quotes from several companies so that you can compare and negotiate prices.

2. VERIFY LICENSING

Make sure the moving company is licensed, bonded, and insured. Interstate movers are licensed by the Federal Motor Carrier Safety Administration. On their website you'll find more information on screening movers suitably:

- protectyourmove.gov

To run a thorough vetting of the mover, go to:

- Better Business Bureau at bbb.org
- American Moving & Storage Association at moving.org

3. AVOID CASH PAYMENTS AND LARGE DEPOSITS

If you deposit more than 20 percent or pay in cash, you are vulnerable. The move may go well, but it might not. Better to pay using a credit card that protects you in case something goes wrong.

4. VERIFY INSURANCE

Accredited movers carry a basic insurance policy that is sufficient if something gets broken or lost. They also offer a higher-level replacement coverage for an additional charge. Ask how much is covered under the basic policy, and decide if the higher level is worth the cost. Also be sure to check your homeowner's policy that may cover lost or damaged items.

5. READ THE CONTRACT THOROUGHLY

Read the full agreement, including the fine print, to ensure that it contains all vital information and is accurate. Don't sign anything unless you're satisfied and understand it all. And never sign an incomplete or blank contract, even if it's from a reputable company. Never sign a document releasing a mover from liability for missing or damaged items. If you have any questions, ask them before the move.

Your Senior Move Manager will be an invaluable ally in making sure all five of these protections are in place and working to your benefit.

Senior Move Managers can bring in resources

As you work with a Senior Move Manager, you'll find they have partnerships with other professionals who help in downsizing. Expect them to team up with professionals who care about handling a senior relocation with compassion and understanding, ensuring a well-organized transition. These pros may include the following:

☐ Specialty Moving Contractors
☐ Hauling/Junk Removal Companies
☐ Handymen and Cleaning Services
☐ Remodeling Contractors
☐ Financial Planners
☐ Real Estate Downsizing Professionals
☐ Elder Law and Estate Attorneys
☐ Home Healthcare Professionals
☐ Medical Equipment Specialists
☐ Senior Placement Agents

This last professional, the Senior Placement Agent, becomes important when a senior no longer wishes, or is no longer able, to move to another private house. This professional helps with the decision about the community living arrangement that will be best for the next chapter in life. And indeed, it's the next chapter in this book.

4

Senior Placement Agents

HIGHLIGHTS

▶ Working with a Senior Placement Agent

▶ Selecting the best Senior Placement Agent near you

▶ Costs of assisted living facilities

▶ Living options available to you

"Mom insists that she's fine," Lee said, leading off the Zoom call with his three younger siblings, all of them in their sixties now.

"But I just left the house," Bryan spoke next. "I gave her the 'draw a clock' test to check for cognition. Gave her a pencil and a piece of paper with a circle drawn in the middle, and asked her to draw in a clock with the time being ten minutes after 11, like the experts advise."

"And she agreed to that?" Craig's surprise was obvious.

"She did it, and got the 1–12 right, but drew only the big hand, not the little hand, though I waited for her to. So yeah, she's slipped."

"She raised us in that home, and she should stay there if she wants," Doreen finally weighed in, clearly edgy.

"Did I mention she's stopped showering—"

"Come on, Bryan, she fell and broke her wrist but popped right back after surgery. She's safe at home, that's what matters, right?

"But she still has her hobbies; she's still playing bridge."

"That's just it. I think she's mostly suffering from loneliness. If she were in one of those retirement communities, she might love it."

"And it might help us avoid moving her into a nursing home after a 911 call."

"But change can be so difficult for her."

"As it would be, will be, for any of us."

"How about bringing in someone who can talk with her about all this?" Lee asked. "Might be the right first step."

It can be difficult for adult children, especially in larger families, to grapple with the decline of a parent's health and the next best steps to take. It can be even more difficult when the children now live far from a parent requiring care. Having an ally in the process can be the most helpful thing.

These allies are known as Senior Placement Agents, and they can help with every step. The services of these agents are typically compensated by the assisted living facilities, so they are free to you. For your reference, these agents are usually paid a flat fee or a commission by the assisted living facility they place an individual with. So it's very important to select an agent who is trustworthy and eager to point out all your available options, basically taking a big burden off of you, and earning the fees they are paid.

There are also Senior Placement Agents that are compensated by the senior or family that is needing the service. In not being compensated by the senior community itself, they are able to remain as impartial as possible in the selection of the senior community.

Selecting the best Senior Placement Agent near you

There are several organizations that offer accreditation for Senior Placement Agents, and it's wise to select an agent listed by one of these groups.

The Society of Certified Senior Advisors is a first-rate group in my experience, since they first educate and then certify professionals to work with seniors. To obtain a Certified Senior Advisor (CSA) credential, the professional has to demonstrate competence in working with older adults, agree to a Code of Professional Responsibility, and complete an ethics course.

- To learn more about Certified Senior Advisors, go to: csa.us.
- To find a CSA near you, go to: portal.csa.us/csa-locator.

Another good source for Senior Placement Agents is the National Placement Referral Alliance. See their listings at npralliance.org.

Working with a Senior Placement Agent

Every Senior Placement Agent will have their own approach, seeking to distinguish themselves in the marketplace, but they all go through a similar four-step process to ensure a safe, quality placement for the senior and peace of mind for the whole family:

1. UNDERSTAND THE SENIOR'S NEEDS

To begin with, a Senior Placement Agent will ask some questions about the senior's health condition and particular needs. This will help them assess the senior's situation so that they can make the best recommendations for the care needed and the facilities for the next stage of life. Expect to talk about the following:

- ☐ *Medical history*—What health conditions exist, such as chronic illnesses or disabilities, diabetes, Parkinson's, or Alzheimer's? In addition, what current medications are being taken?
- ☐ *Allergies and dietary restrictions*—Are there allergies to certain foods or dietary restrictions or a diet based on personal or religious preferences?
- ☐ *Preferred location*—Where ideally should the facility be located? Near to the current home, to family, to an area with special meaning?
- ☐ *Personal services needed*—What kind of daily assistance will be needed for tasks such as bathing, dressing, or walking?
- ☐ *Religious and cultural preferences*—Is there a preference for a faith-based community or a cultural community with residents of the same background?
- ☐ *Amenities desired*—What kinds of activities and entertainment would make the facility more fulfilling?
- ☐ *Preferred size of community*—Is the desire to be in a smaller setting or a larger community? What is the ideal number of residents they'd want to reside among?

☐ *Budget and financial needs*—To make sure the facility search is held within a price range and to offer recommendations on financial help.

With this information, the Senior Placement Agent can determine which community best matches these needs and desires.

2. MATCH TO SOME COMMUNITY OPTIONS

Matching an individual with the right assisted living option brings many factors into play: location, cost, current and future care requirements, amenities, pricing, occupancy rates, number of residents, resident-to-staff ratios, proximity to hospitals, facility reviews, and more.

Finding all this information on your own can be a daunting task. But a good Senior Placement Agent will have it at the ready. And within days of your first inquiry, you should be given a list of options to consider.

These discussions can be hard ones for everyone in the family, which can often lead to frictions between the senior and the adult family members.

Which brings up the next step.

3. ARRANGE TOURS OF THE COMMUNITIES

Before making any decision about a community, you'll want to tour the facilities first. These personal tours are a time-consuming, often emotionally taxing, but necessary part of the process. So your Senior Placement Agent should try to decrease the number of tours scheduled to two or three. There may be five to seven in the area of choice, but begin with fewer. Then if you don't have a fit, you can always widen the filter to look at more communities.

Your Senior Placement Agent should accompany you on these tours, knowing what to ask and look for. Of course, you can arrange to go on your own if more to your choosing.

Ideally take the time to have a meal at each community you visit, to get a feel for the quality of food and day-to-day environment.

Before any choice of communities is made, your Senior Placement Agent should ensure that all the appropriate questions have been asked and answered. They should advocate on the senior's behalf, be there to help you negotiate the best terms with your chosen facility, and assist with all the details of moving in.

4. FOLLOW UP ON THE CHOSEN COMMUNITY

Once a community is chosen, a good Senior Placement Agent should still be there for you. They should work with the movers to ensure that all the right furniture and belongings are moved into the new living space, just the way the senior wants it.

The best agents I've worked with do a follow-up visit a few days after moving in to check on the transition to the new life. Lastly, the agent will check in at least once more after a month to make sure the senior is adjusting well to the new environment, happy and satisfied.

With the right Senior Placement Agent in your corner, the entire family will feel confident in the continued care of a loved one.

Cost of assisted living communities

Naturally, the cost of assisted living varies from state to state and from community to community. Some communities bill on an inclusive basis, meaning the fees include the room and all care services. Others offer a pick of services on an à la carte basis. Your Senior Placement

Agent can help you (a) find the right priced options for communities in your area and (b) negotiate the best price possible in the community you ultimately select.

Type of Care	Monthly	Annual
In-home Caregiver (44 hours a week)	$4,000	$48,000
In-home Caregiver (full time)	$10,000	$120,000
Independent Living Community	$4,000	$48,000
Assisted Living Community	$5,000	$60,000
Skilled Nursing Facility	$8,000	$96,000
Memory Care Facility	$7,000	$84,000

There are as many kinds of assisted living options as there are companies offering solutions in the fast-growing elder care industry. These assisted living options are easiest to understand when put into five big categories:

1. AN INDEPENDENT LIVING COMMUNITY

Independent living communities are designed for seniors who want to live in their own home or apartment within a shared complex—featuring social interaction with peers, stimulating activities both inside and out of the community, physical and educational activities—while being free of the everyday tasks like housekeeping, laundry, grocery shopping, meal prep, and even driving.

Top-quality communities of this type tend to fill up fast and have years-long waiting lists, so it's good to start planning for this early.

Accommodations vary in size, from suites to 1+-bedroom apartments with kitchens. Pets are usually welcome, even encouraged. The big emphasis in these independent living communities is social interaction with fellow seniors. It can offer an improved quality of life, which can also lessen depression-related health issues.

Seniors can enjoy typically first-rate meals in either the dining room or the privacy of their apartment. Almost every community offers amenities like on-site beauty salons, libraries, theaters, billiards rooms, woodworking shops, classes on lots of subjects and hobbies, cards, and board games. And when that's not enough, there's always available transport to off-site events and appointments.

Along with trained medical teams, there's an added sense of security and safety with emergency call buttons in the units. If there's a sudden need for assistance, it's just a push button away. And if the senior doesn't show up for regular activities, there's a friendly aide who pays them a visit to make sure all is well.

2. AN ASSISTED LIVING COMMUNITY

In assisted living communities, there's a higher level of supervision than in independent living communities but not as intensive as a nursing home.

Apartments vary in size from studios to 1+-bedroom apartment designs.

Services include health and wellness programs, medication management, bathing, toileting, dressing, cognitive support, assistance with transfers, and the like.

Assisted living communities tend toward a campus- or hotel-like feel, with light or full housekeeping, laundry service, and nice dining rooms offering delicious food with waiters taking meal orders. Other amenities include beauty salons, gyms, pools, libraries, and entertainment, as well as transportation to outside events, such as the symphony, movie theaters, shopping, and other activities.

There's also twenty-four-hour security to ensure the resident's safety and well-being.

A common misconception is that assisted living communities are filled with people who sit around in silence, which is nowhere close to reality. Most residents are independent in body and spirit. Many just need a little more help than was available for them at home.

Many communities offer short-term respite care for those recovering from a procedure or when a primary caregiver needs a break from twenty-four-hour care.

Another type of assisted living is a residential care home, or "board and care" homes as they are known. These are smaller homes ideal for seniors who desire more one-on-one attention since these homes are typically limited to six or seven residents. They are beautiful and homey settings providing a family environment. Many are set up so that residents don't have to move again and can comfortably age in place with the support of end-of-life hospice care, if needed.

All communities are monitored and regulated by their states to various degrees, and reports on them can be obtained for added peace of mind.

3. SKILLED NURSING FACILITIES

When twenty-four-hour care becomes essential, and the family can no longer manage an in-home solution, a nursing home becomes the best option.

Also known as skilled nursing facilities, rest homes, long-term care facilities, and convalescent homes, residents here have their own private room or share a room, depending on financial and health factors. All needed services, including medical and rehab therapies, are provided.

Residents may be fully or partially mobile or may be restricted to a chair or a bed. A doctor's help in deciding to use a skilled nursing facility is well advised.

4. MEMORY CARE COMMUNITIES

When a senior's mental health deteriorates significantly, a memory care community can be the best next step. These communities are specifically designed for people with Alzheimer's or other forms of dementia.

The building designs include single-level private and semi-private rooms. Often, semi-private rooms are preferred to help offset the loneliness and isolation that occur naturally. There are alarms on the windows and doors to prevent wandering. There are no stairs, for ease of walking about. Center courtyards are enclosed so that residents may take in fresh air and sunshine while still staying safe and secure.

A lower staff-to-resident ratio is common in these communities. But the staff there are specially trained to care for seniors who can exhibit what are called "advanced stage" behaviors, such as aggression, depression, and confusion.

The same medical care as nursing homes is offered, with some additional safety precautions to protect residents. Services include restaurant-style meals served three times a day, on-site medical care, assistance with daily activities such as grooming and dressing, linen and laundry services, and 24/7 security.

5. CONTINUING CARE RETIREMENT COMMUNITIES

For the greatest flexibility in living options, people choose continuing care retirement communities. Included in these communities is the full range of options that residents might need. From independent living to assisted living to skilled nursing and long-term care facilities, all on the same property.

Senior Placement Agents bring in other resources

By its very nature, the downsizing community includes professionals in all the various aspects of care providing. So a Senior Placement Agent will have a network of relationships they trust and can rely on to extend their expertise beyond their immediate specialty. This network can include the following:

- ☐ Elder Law and Estate Attorneys
- ☐ Veterans Assistance Providers
- ☐ Senior Move Managers and Moving Companies
- ☐ Construction Contractors
- ☐ Real Estate Downsizing Professionals
- ☐ Medical Equipment Specialists
- ☐ Fiduciary Financial Planners
- ☐ Home Healthcare Agencies

And when it comes time to leave the home, whenever that is, the goal will likely be to raise as much money as possible to prepare for the next chapter in life. And that's why we'll talk next about estate sales and auction houses.

5

Estate Sales/ Auction Professionals

HIGHLIGHTS

► Holding a tasteful, successful estate sale

► Making the most of an estate auction

► Auction or estate sale, which is better for your family?

"All of Mom and Dad's stuff will be worth a small fortune if we sell it," Robert kicked off the Zoom call with his two siblings.

"But we're not going to sell it," Judy practically cut him off. "This is their life, all their memories, our memories. I'm not going to let some stranger go rummaging through them!"

"So, what, we stick it all in a storage unit nobody ever visits?" Robert asked. "Though we keep paying for it month after month?"

"You two are not making this any easier," Josette put in. "But for once I agree with Judy, we can't just cast off their forty-eight years together in forty-eight hours."

"But we have expenses, costs of closing out the home, and we've already claimed the items we each want. So why not unload the rest of the stuff with ..."

"Dignity?"

"Yes, with the dignity that Mom and Dad deserve!"

"I say we sell what we can, donate what we can, and dump the rest."

"That's cold, Robert."

"No, that's me being rational."

And on the Zoom call went for a several-hour-long emotional roller coaster, ending only once they all three hung up on one another.

Dealing with a family estate is never easy and rarely fun. But I've found that if a family agrees to agree on two things from the outset, the process will unfold more lovingly and successfully. It can even turn into a celebration of a loved one's life, as it should be.

1. *Take it slow.* Give everyone time to grieve in their own way and to come around to the decision-making after having spent time thinking about it.

2. *Enlist help.* Talk to estate professionals who have no vested interest in your stuff. They are in the best position to neutralize family tensions if they exist. They have deep domain expertise in the estate market and can tell you right away

what your best course of action may be when you're ready to act.

These professionals can also hook you up with an appraiser who can come in and give you some financial data to work with. That'll help the family figure out what approach makes the most sense. Appraiser fees vary by region and experience but range from $125 to $300 per hour. Or if you go directly to an estate sales or auction company, they'll have qualified appraisers on staff.

Be sure to check an appraiser's credentials. You're looking for accreditations from the American Society of Appraisers, International Society of Appraisers, or Appraisers Association of America. Ask how long they've been at it. Experience really pays dividends in this line of work, even with the internet offering a trove of information on everything under the sun.

Also, it's not usually wise to hire an appraiser who charges a percentage of the appraised value, since it creates a conflict of interest. Instead, pay outright. It's a good investment. Your appraiser will evaluate your valuables for tax and sales purposes and issue a full report.

Even before hiring an estate sales or auction company, there are things to do first:

- ☐ Remove all important papers from the house for safekeeping.
- ☐ If there are rare books or collectibles that might find a home with a known seller or friend, see what interest there is. Artifacts may interest a local museum.
- ☐ If there are only a few valuable items to sell, try eBay. High-end, brand-name products tend to do well there. And eBay has a handy tool for telling you what similar items are selling for.

(eBay and PayPal take a combined 13 percent cut, plus factor in shipping costs.)

☐ Lower-value or bulky goods are good candidates for Craigslist. Holding a yard sale may also be worthwhile for unloading such items.

☐ Consignment shops are an alternative for selling furniture, antiques, clothing, and other items. They typically display your goods on the floor for thirty to ninety days and take 50 percent of whatever sells.

☐ Giving belongings that are in good condition to your favorite charity can save you the hassle of trying to sell them. (See donationtown.org for charities by location that will pick up donations.)

☐ If you itemize deductions on your taxes, don't forget to get a receipt for charitable donations. You'll have to give a description of donations valued at $500+ on IRS Form 8283. Donated items worth $5,000+ require a formal appraisal to include on your tax return.

If your possessions to be disposed of are worth $10,000 or more, then an estate sale or auction company will be interested in working with you.

Holding a tasteful, successful estate sale

Estate sales are usually held at the home to sell off the personal property within the home. Folks in the industry like to say they are driven by the four Ds—death, divorce, downsizing, and debt. Sounds cold, but they are generally a good bunch to work with.

An estate sale is an excellent way to clear out large amounts of items in a short period of time—typically two to three days. Proceeds can be used to pay off debts and distribute to the heirs. Estate sales are a convenient way to reach a large number of buyers seeking antiques, paintings, and family treasures for a great deal.

In fact, estate sales are booming in America. With 10,000 baby boomers turning sixty-five each day, there are an estimated $3 million worth of family possessions being sold each day at estate sales, with nearly 117,000 companies involved in this business nationwide.[12]

Because of the nontechnical nature of this business, many people are tempted to host their own estate sales. It's certainly doable, but there are more details to get right than first meet the eye. A lot of sweat equity goes into estate liquidations. And for the amateur, there's a good chance of being ripped off, burned out, sent to the chiropractor, or all three.

An estate sale company will generally charge a guaranteed minimum of $1,500 against a commission of 35–50 percent that they'll take from gross sales.[13] Plus there is also a cleanout fee, charged at an hourly rate. Such a hefty commission and fees often surprise families, but there is a lot of work involved in running a proper estate sale. And there is the luxury of letting somebody else handle things— when it can be hard for some family members to let go.

These estate professionals also often have connections with regular buyers of antiques and can help get better prices for select objects than you could. They will price items to get the most they think possible—since their interests are aligned with yours in that way. They will also set up your home so that the items for sale are visually appealing and safe from breakage as buyers pass through. A staff member or two will be there controlling the crowd and keeping an eye out for thieves while running the cashier stand.

Estate sale proceeds are not usually subject to income tax. However, there may be some restrictions on what you can do with the estate's money. To avoid problems, you should consult a tax professional or attorney.

When time comes to select an estate sale company, you have many options.

Be sure to interview a handful of companies before selecting your finalist. Ask about their services, prices, and insurance. Ask them to come to the house to meet with you, and look things over and offer a preliminary assessment of what you should be able to attain from an estate sale. This initial consultation should be free of charge.

Once an estate sale company is retained, they will come in to formally assess, sort, clean, price, and tag items. They may also bring in appraisers to get pricing right. They will set up and conduct the sale—at the house or online, your choice. It will run for two to three days. And they should help you handle the items that remain afterward through donation, recycling, or disposal. Finally, they'll clean up your house, tally up the sales proceeds, deduct their commission, and give you a check with a sales report and tax donation receipts.

Making the most of an estate auction

Estate auctions differ slightly from estate sales in the way prices are set. In an auction, the group of bidders who shows up gets to decide the price for an item based on the demand for it. The family can set a minimum price, but otherwise the bidders place their bids until one wins. So, a popular item can sell for far more than expected. Or the opposite can happen, and an item doesn't sell at all.

Typically, an auction service will come to your home and take items to a gallery to sell along with other goods. If you have enough high-value items, an auctioneer may host an on- or off-site auction of your items. Commissions range from 10 to 25 percent of the so-called hammer price but may shoot as high as 50 percent.[14] Plus, there can be additional fees for transportation, storage, and marketing.

So how to decide between an auction and a sale?

You will learn a lot in talking to both estate sales and auction professionals, and often one company will do both, so they are incentivized to steer you in the direction that benefits all parties. But to help you decide, think about the following:

☐ How valuable are the items in the estate?

☐ Do these items have any historical or cultural significance?

☐ How many items are there, and how will they handle being transported?

☐ Is it more important to get the highest possible value for each item, or is it more important to sell as many items as possible?

If you have items of significant historical value, then an auction may be the best course. Also, an auction can help create bidding wars, so you may come away with more proceeds. However, if you have a large number of items in the estate and want to sell as many of them as possible, an estate sale may be the better course.

As I noted, it helps to find an estate sales and auction house professional you are comfortable working with. Talk to them about their services, and get a sense of how they would handle the process. You will come away much more certain of the direction you should take.

To select an estate sales or auction house partner in your area, here are directories to consult:

- estatesales.org
- auctioneers.org

- aselonline.com
- estatesales.net

Auction or estate sale, which is better for your family?

PROS	
Estate Sale	**Estate Auction**
Sell at the house, no need to move items	Can be held at auction house; no strangers in the house
Can last 2-3 days, for more potential buyers	Bidding can lead to higher selling prices
Creates illusion of scarcity which can lift prices	Online and absentee bidding can result in more buyers
CONS	
Estate Sale	**Estate Auction**
Takes some time to select items to prepare for the sale	One-day event limits buyer attendance
Strangers haggling over your loved one's possessions	Off-site auctions means you pay transportation costs
Might not know value of items until they are sold off	Longer lead times to set up the auction

Whichever you choose, I wish you all the best in handling this sentimental part of the "moving out" process. With it, we are left with only two more key players in downsizing: the elder care and estate attorneys.

6

Elder Care and Estate Attorneys

HIGHLIGHTS

▶ How an elder care attorney can serve you

▶ Using an estate attorney to your fullest advantage

▶ How to find an attorney you can trust

"How do we unload a lifetime of possessions, all that Mom and Dad did for us?"

Joel couldn't reply to his sister Sarah's question because he was still too wracked with grief.

"Joel, we have to sell their condo, go through their stuff, find homes for everything."

Every word his sister had just said sounded unimaginable to Joel, too painful to even approach.

"Joel, I know what you're thinking, or not thinking," Sarah said softly, knowing her brother had always been the emotional one. "But in life pain is inevitable; suffering is an option."

She was right, Joel knew. Logistically, emotionally, they needed to sort it out. Needed to honor Mom and Dad.

Sarah knew that, too. "We'll honor Mom and Dad, Joel."

It can be difficult, when emotions are running high over a parent's declining health or their passing, to keep a clear head about things. Difficult to even know where to turn for help in understanding what to do next. What logistically you need to do, what legally you need to do.

If you've heard of elder care attorneys and estate planning attorneys but aren't really sure what the differences are and how it matters, you are not alone.

Elder care and estate attorneys are quite similar in that both areas of the law ideally involve planning for the future. But they are different in that elder law focuses on protecting your assets while you are still alive, while estate planning usually centers around what happens after you pass away.

So there is overlap. And it is common for attorneys to practice both elder care and estate planning. But in selecting an attorney, you need to be careful to select one that fits your needs.

- ☐ *Seek an elder care attorney* when you begin anticipating the need for long-term care for a loved one and are wondering how to pay for that care.
- ☐ *Seek an estate attorney* early in your retirement years to make sure you maximize your financial position, are set to pay for

the long-term care you may need, can smoothly hand over a business you may want to remain in the family, and distribute your wealth to those whom you love.

How an elder law attorney can serve you

Elder law attorneys specialize in the legal needs of elderly people, veterans, and adults with special needs. This is a new area of law born out of necessity. We are living longer and having to deal with illnesses, diseases, and rising healthcare costs in later years. Elder law attorneys can provide guidance and advice in dealing with all the complexities of this aging process.

They can help find nursing homes and long-term care when needed.

They can assist in obtaining government funds to pay for it all, completing and filing the forms that are required for this assistance.

If a family member becomes incapacitated, they can help set up power of attorney capabilities.

If a family member can no longer care for themselves, elder care attorneys can help set up a family member or trusted friend as a guardian (known as adult guardianship) and then help that guardian handle the role properly.

All of these later-life decisions can be overwhelming for the very reason that they do involve intimate life and death issues. But as we age, we must get our affairs in order. And sort out our estates. And take proper care of our loved ones. And hold onto our own independence as long as we gracefully can. That's the path, and elder law attorneys are there to guide, educate, and walk us through things like wills, trust planning, setting up a power of attorney, and qualifying for government benefits to help pay for long-term care costs instead of letting it deplete the savings.

Certainly, there are online resources now that help with the basics of will preparation, trusts, and other aging issues. If the estate is simple, these online resources can be money-saving approaches. But if the estate is at all complex, as we'll see, the one-size-fits-all estate planning services can be penny wise and pound foolish. They can create some big problems for you down the road and for your family and heirs.

Elder care attorneys with experience have seen the kinds of financial and medical situations that seniors can encounter. This gives them valuable insight into the range of options in long-term care so that you can be well prepared for what lies ahead.

Most common reasons people contact elder care attorneys

☐ Have an incapacitated spouse in need of long-term care

☐ Have an estate that is taxable and needs managing

☐ Have a second marriage or more

☐ Have lost a spouse or other family member recently

☐ Have no children, minor children, or problem children

☐ Have at least one business they own

☐ Have property owned in another state

Long-term care planning

Families are frequently divided over caring for their parents. An elder care attorney can offer an impartial, objective opinion about the best long-term plan for the parent. Often a parent will want to stay at home, but that's not the safest, smartest choice any longer. An elder care attorney can recommend the best strategies for ensuring that an aging loved one is protected.

When a loved one is suffering from a terrible illness, it's natural to wonder and worry about how best to handle their care. An elder law attorney works with you to prepare what's known as a "durable power of attorney." This allows you to make medical or financial decisions on behalf of your loved one when they become incapacitated.

If you neglect to set up a power of attorney in time, and a parent becomes incapacitated, an elder care attorney can still begin guardianship proceedings so that you can handle your loved one's personal and financial affairs.

Should you attempt to handle these legal issues on your own, without an elder care attorney's help, you may be just fine. But you may just as easily lose control of your family's assets to a state-appointed executor, or to the IRS, or to an ex-spouse depending on the situation you're facing.

Every state has their own specific laws on elder care. Some states restrict what can be included in a power of attorney, an advanced healthcare directive, a will, or a trust. Other states limit who can actually take on power of attorney responsibility, so it's important to have the right legal representation to avoid potential mistakes at both the state and the federal levels.

Obtaining government benefits

As I've noted, Medicare does not cover long-term care needs. But Medicaid does cover some costs on a means-tested basis. That means applicants must have very limited assets and income to qualify.

Many people right away think they can qualify for these Medicaid funds if they just give away their assets to family members or others, in hopes of showing low-enough assets to qualify them for Medicaid assistance.

But both state and federal programs look back at finances for five years when they're deciding on eligibility. And if money is "spent down," as they call it, then the applicant will be penalized for a period of time, disqualified from the program, and forced to pay for care out of pocket.

This is where legal and financial strategies can be set up by an elder care attorney to help the family meet as many of these long-term care needs as possible.

For veterans, there is also help available through a program known as the Aid and Attendance benefit. These funds can be used to offset the cost of long-term care.[15]

DON'T REGRET IT LATER!

Failing to prepare means preparing to fail when it comes to wills. Neglect it, and the state will determine who inherits your assets (automobiles, property, savings accounts, everything).

Offering financial advice

Your goal is always to make the most of your retirement years with the wealth you have, and an elder care attorney and an estate attorney can help in a number of ways.

You want to make sure you are minimizing gift taxes, estate taxes, and income taxes on anything you transfer over to a loved one.

And if you own a business that you want to keep operating after you pass, the estate needs to be properly structured for it.

There are quite a lot of tax-wise moves, depending on your financial picture, that a savvy attorney can help with. So selecting a good attorney is very important.

Using an estate attorney to your fullest advantage

Many people think estate planning is for the rich. Not at all. Estate planning is really nothing more than a map for your future. How do you want to address your personal needs and desires in terms of retirement, distribute your wealth to those whom you love, or hand over a business you may want to remain in the family?

Since none of us knows what the future holds, preparing for the contingencies is part of being a responsible adult. Perhaps you need help planning your own estate, or you're helping a family member plan theirs. The critical thing is to consult with an estate attorney before life's events force you onto emergency footing. You don't want that.

> ## DON'T REGRET IT LATER!
>
> Letting an estate plan slip can cause giant problems. Suppose a couple sold their estate to pay for a move into a retirement community, but then the husband passed away soon after. The remainder of the inheritance funds could end up in the hands of a child from a previous marriage. The wife could be left without means because the estate plan was not properly updated.

Preparing a will properly

If you do nothing else, at least have your final wishes known about how to handle your assets. Ideally, you'll make this known even before you officially begin retirement.

Wait too long—that is, if you haven't put a plan in place—then your family could be forced into an estate sale or auction by the courts. It's not a comfortable place to be. Similarly, if a confusing will is left behind, the heirs soon learn, they could be forced to liquidate the estate in order to divide up their inheritances more efficiently.

Setting up the right kind of trust

A trust is something you put in place while you're still alive to protect your assets and shape your legacy as you wish it to be.

A trust can be used during your lifetime to support your financial needs in a tax advantaged manner. A trust can cover the costs of long-term care, and then when you pass, the balance of the funds can go to the beneficiaries you have chosen.

Trusts are managed by a trustee, and selecting the right trustee for you can be tricky. If you choose a family member or friend, that person has to be trustworthy and fully up to the task with the financial know-how. If, on the contrary, you choose a professional, you will pay fees for this service which range from 0.5 to 2 percent of the asset value of the trust.[16] An intermediate option that many consider is a co-trustee where a family member shares the responsibility with a professional, for the greater peace of mind that can bring.

A big benefit of a trust is that you avoid probate, which means your assets can be distributed to your heirs more quickly. And trusts can be kept private in a way that a regular will cannot be since wills are entered into the public record.

An estate attorney can guide you to the best trust for your situation, making sure that your document is well structured and legally binding. There are many kinds of trusts, with each attempting to accomplish a specific goal you may have. Clearly, there are a lot of questions to be answered in properly fashioning a trust. And relying on legal counsel to guide you through the right steps for you just makes sense.

How to find an attorney you can trust

Estate planning is so easy to put off, and then put off some more, because it forces us to contemplate financial issues that will occur while we're living and then after we pass. Yet we want to make sure that our estate is managed prudently, that the next generation receives the inheritance they deserve without misfortune.

Any attorney or online legal service can draw up a simple will for straightforward situations, such as naming a beneficiary for your 401(k). But only a seasoned estate attorney should be trusted to navigate more complicated situations that involve multiple trusts or multiple heirs, uncertainty about trustees, or tax deferral issues.

In looking for the best elder care or estate attorney for you:

☐ Seek recommendations from family, friends, and associates.

☐ Ask your accountant, financial advisor, or state bar association for a referral.

☐ To search online in your area, go to:

 ▫ National Elder Law Foundation

 ▫ National Association of Estate Planners & Councils

☐ Get referrals from local agencies who work with seniors, such as the Alzheimer's Association, AARP, and hospital social workers.

☐ Your local Agency on Aging also lists low-cost and free legal services.

It's always smart to interview a couple of different attorneys to make sure you find one you are comfortable with. Here are some good questions to ask, as well as observations to make, about your candidates:

- *First and foremost, is the attorney a compassionate person?* This becomes very important when the family is experiencing a significant loss. Do you feel the attorney could come alongside you in a difficult time, easing you through legal issues in a caring way? Personal issues are going to come up. Are you comfortable discussing sensitive, private matters with this attorney?

- *Is the attorney board-certified in elder care or estate law?* Is that a specialization, and are they current on the legal statutes so that they can carefully word your documents in the most effective way possible?

- *Has the attorney had any problems?* Any warnings, disbarments, or sanctions against them in your state or another state?

- *Are there any ethical issues?* Does the attorney have any conflicts of interest with spouses or children? And if there are potential conflicts, have you discussed them, and do you understand them?

- *How much will it cost?* Ask about fees and expenses at the initial consultation. Attorneys cannot provide a complete quote until they study your particular situation, but they can offer a range of fees for their services. Some attorneys charge flat fees for this work instead of billing by the hour. A regular estate planning document, for reference, can range in cost from a few hundred dollars to a few thousand dollars, depending on the complexity of the estate.

- *Does the attorney actually execute an estate plan?* Some attorneys only draw up estate plans, while others execute the trusts as well. It's usually better to retain an attorney who ensures that the correct assets go into the trust.

- *What is the attorney's estate tax experience?* The government changes tax laws fairly regularly, and you want an attorney who is current on the laws so that you avoid all the taxes you can.

- *How long will it take?* Usually there will be no rush to complete an estate plan, but you want to leave time to discuss your plan with an accountant or a financial advisor. Give yourself enough time to fully understand your estate plan and what's involved in implementing it.

- *Are there others in the office available to you?* It's important to know that an associate or paralegal will be there for your questions in an emergency if your lawyer is not available.

All of your questions should be handled along with the statement of work to be done in the engagement letter the attorney gives you at the outset of the retainer.

Elder care and estate attorneys have many resources

Your attorney will have relationships with other professionals involved in senior downsizing. They can make introductions to people they trust in a number of areas:

- ☐ Medical Social Workers
- ☐ Home Healthcare Professionals
- ☐ Senior Placement Agents
- ☐ Senior Community Managers
- ☐ Financial Planners
- ☐ Real Estate Downsizing Professionals

And with this, we've covered all the professionals who can help with the "move out" in the downsizing process. We turn now to those who can help with the "move in."

PART II

Professionals Who Help with Moving In

Senior Community Managers

"Can't judge a book by its cover, or these retirement homes by their soothing pink exteriors and lush gardens," Adrienne told her husband. "If you could judge by the outside, they're all slices of heaven. But they're not. I watch the news. I know some of these places just don't measure up."

Paul didn't interrupt his wife, knowing to let this rant run its course. Truth be told, he was just as worried about putting Adrienne's mother into a home in their Houston suburb. Even a home he'd driven by for years. Because he'd never gone into one himself and had no idea what it was really like.

"But Mom can't stay on her own in that old house," Adrienne continued, "or the next time she leaves the gas stove running, she'll burn the house down around her."

Again, thought Paul, a little overdramatic. But he and Adrienne were about to depart on a year-long boat cruise on the inland passageway. They obviously couldn't leave until Mom was settled somewhere safe.

"But where Paul, where will she go!?"

———— 🏠 ————

As we talked about earlier, two out of three older Americans will relocate in their later years.[17] And for many of us, the next step will be a senior living community. That could be independent living in a gated community or in a monitored nursing home or in a memory care facility. While each of these facilities is different, the people in charge of them are quite similar in the primary role they play: ensuring a high level of care for our loved ones at this stage in life.

The two most important individuals you'll meet in these communities are the Executive Manager and the Marketing Manager. They set the tone for the quality of the community. Let's look at them.

Judging a community by its Executive Manager

Whether the title is Executive Manager or Director, this person oversees the day-to-day operations and is ultimately responsible for all who work in the community. That can include a wellness director, caregivers, physician assistants and nurses, social workers, a dining manager, wait staff, an activities director, and drivers as well as the behind-the-scenes people.

In a smaller community, the Executive Manager may wear two hats and handle marketing duties as well.

A good executive is going to foster a positive and supportive working environment, taking care to recruit and train a team that shares a commitment to providing top-quality care in a nurturing, home-like environment. This is not always easily done, because the executive must also control costs to maximize the net operating income of the facility. This often requires trade-offs, and an adept executive will find a balance that meets the community's financial goals while upholding a reputation in the area as a safe and secure place where the residents thrive.

Assisted living is a highly regulated industry, and the executive is responsible for making sure the community and its workers follow the laws and remain in compliance with regulations at the federal, state, and local levels.

This means making sure that the staff always meets the residents' needs in a timely fashion. This involves all kinds of technical factors such as staffing ratios, bed capacity, housekeeping and sanitation, food services, and the like. But in direct resident satisfaction terms, it means the following:

- ☐ Cultivating a team of caregivers dedicated to the residents' needs
- ☐ Supervising the kitchen crew to meet meal needs and dietary restrictions
- ☐ Planning recreational activities, including daily activities and optional events
- ☐ Connecting with families on their loved one's resident health and wellness
- ☐ Leading the community staff to ensure that operations run efficiently

This is the executive at work. You're more likely to meet this individual after you've met the community's Marketing Manager.

Key role played by the Marketing Manager

Whatever the size of the community, the Marketing Manager's job can be the trickiest: to keep the rooms in the community as fully occupied as possible while at the same time not "overselling" or "pressuring" a family into signing up if the community is not right for them.

Good Marketing Managers handle this by giving first-rate tours of their facilities and letting those tours do the "selling."

These communities also run outreach and advertising campaigns to generate interest, and the Marketing Manager is responsible for running these campaigns in a respectful but effective manner. That is, if the outreach you see is creative and optimistic, you can hope that the living conditions are, as well.

As noted, the Marketing Manager is likely the first person you'll see since they are in charge of giving tours.

Touring a senior community

When I first visited a living community for someone close to my family, I felt like I was walking into an entire new world. The place could actually have doubled for a nice hotel, from the looks of it. But I knew I had to ask the right questions and look beyond first appearances to make the best decision for my family.

I did my homework going in so that I had a lot of questions ready to ask on the tour. I've recreated it here for you so that your every concern can be anticipated.

WHAT DO YOU OBSERVE RIGHT AWAY?

Does the community feel small or large to you, and how will it feel to your loved one? Are the hallways wide and elevators easily accessed so that "getting around" is not an issue? Is the staff keeping the place clean, with lots of flowers and colorful accents as well as good mood lighting? Does it smell pleasant in all areas? Are the common areas, dining room, and hallways looking tidy? Are the outdoor areas inviting and safe-looking?

These are the things you notice right off. Then you begin looking closer.

Do the residents look well groomed, with reasonably good hygiene? Grooming isn't about fashion, of course. It's about how cared-for the residents feel and are. You want your loved one to look forward to the day, dressing to engage with their new friends and excited about the day's activities. Grooming is an important part of that.

Look at the details, such as windows and furnishings. Are they well kept? That's a sign of attention to detail, and that matters. Ask to see a room like one your loved one would have. What's the view from the window? Are the decor and colors going to uplift your loved one's mood each day?

WHEN'S THE BEST TIME TO TAKE A TOUR?

As you research the community options in your target area, and narrow your options down to a handful, plan to make several visits to these communities at different times of day.

In the morning, are the residents awake and dressed? Even those who need help with basic care or who are experiencing memory loss should be treated with the dignity they deserve. You will see that best early in the day. Of course, this isn't always easy with every resident. But if generally the residents do not look well groomed, this could be a sign of neglected caregiving in other areas.

Around midday, are the residents up and about? It's normal for the elderly to nap more, of course, but they should not be sleeping through the day because they are bored. They should be engaged in activities throughout the day. If it's sunny out, they should be out enjoying the fresh air. Look at the calendar of events to see the activities going on throughout the day.

In the early evening, are the residents interacting with one another around the dinner table? Join in a meal. Taste the quality and menu varieties. See how fresh and nutritious the plates are. Watch the wait staff to see what kind of experience your loved one will be having.

IS THE STAFF FRIENDLY, CAPABLE, AND ENGAGED?

A good community will have one or two people on staff who seem to know everyone, who are always making them laugh or simply showing the kindness of friendship. This can be very important—because this person or persons will be who your loved one sees most often.

Make a point of observing one-on-one interactions between staff and residents to also assess their clinical knowledge about caregiving. You can tell a lot about a caregiver by their understanding of the physical and mental difficulties a resident may be facing.

Learn more about the backgrounds of these caregivers, as well as the facility. See the facility's and staffs' accreditation papers. Ask about ongoing training that they receive.

If extra care is needed for your loved one, ask to speak with the staff who are certified dementia care managers. Ask about the individualized care and treatment plans for similar residents, to see what you can expect. Ask about care for bed-ridden or wheelchair-bound residents. Ask about care for disruptive or aggressive residents. These may not be relevant to your loved one—not yet anyway—but you want to understand how the facility handles these things.

WHAT DO THE RESIDENTS THEMSELVES SAY?

There's no better source than the horse's mouth! Sit down with a couple residents—they'll usually be eager to talk. Ask for their honest opinions—you'll usually get them. Pay close attention to their facial expressions, as well. If they are content with the community, you'll see it in their smiles.

These residents will become your loved one's new friends and daily companions. Do they seem social, engaged, and happy? Join them in a group activity, such as bingo or a social hour, to observe the interactions among them. This socialization is essential to the well-being of seniors.

IS A PRIORITY PUT ON SAFETY AND SECURITY?

Wanting security and safety for a loved one is a common reason for choosing an assisted living community. The living alone, the chance of falling, becoming depressed, having difficulty preparing meals or getting to the store—all are reasons to make the decision. But top of the list has to be security and safety.

So look around the environment for signs of clutter or possible obstructions. There should be nothing to bump into or trip over.

There should be a system in place to handle emergencies when they arise, beginning with an easy-to-use emergency call system. There should be handrails in the hallways. Grab bars in the bathrooms. Seats in the showers. Sprinkler systems throughout the community.

For residents with dementia, it is also helpful to have emergency alert systems, enclosed courtyards, and even color-coded hallways to make navigation easier.

DO YOU UNDERSTAND ALL THE COSTS INVOLVED?

Make sure you understand all the costs and fees, and ask enough questions to clarify the community's billing process and policies.

- ☐ What are the monthly fees?
- ☐ Are the costs all-in covering room, board, and care for a particular level of assistance, or is there an à la carte charge method?
- ☐ What additional charges can be levied?
- ☐ What happens when your loved one needs specialized care?
- ☐ Under what conditions would your loved one be asked to move?
- ☐ Will your loved one need a health assessment before moving in?

Ask for a list of terms and fees, and make sure a detailed breakdown of information is written into your contract.

CAN THE COMMUNITY BE IDEAL FOR YEARS TO COME?

As a loved one's health changes over time, you want to be sure the community has the resources and capabilities to support them. You have to think ahead and decide:

- ☐ Is the community ideal now, or ideal for the longer term, or both?
- ☐ If a move to a greater level of care such as a skilled nursing facility becomes necessary, how will the community help with this transition?
- ☐ No matter the reason for leaving, what type of notice will be required?

FINALLY, WHAT QUESTIONS ARE MOST IMPORTANT TO ASK?

By this point, you should have all the questions you need to ask. But here's a review of the key questions to make sure you're clear. Questions you can put to the community management and staff, as well as the residents, are as follows:

- ☐ What types of living spaces are available?
- ☐ Are there individualized plans for residents?
- ☐ What type of security and safety measures are used?
- ☐ What kinds of medical services are available?
- ☐ Is there a nurse on duty at all times of the day?

☐ How are emergencies handled?

☐ What additional care services are available if needed?

☐ How many staff members care for each resident?

☐ What type of training does the staff complete?

☐ Is transportation readily available?

☐ Is there a full activity and events calendar?

☐ What are the monthly fees and other possible expenses?

☐ Under what circumstances will residents have to move?

Ultimately, you know your loved one best, and you'll have a good intuitive feel about which community is the best fit. And your interactions with the various staff in the community—beginning with the Marketing Manager and the Executive Manager—will help you choose a home that not only caters to your senior's needs but also suits their personality and lifestyle desires.

8

Medical
Social Workers

HIGHLIGHTS

▶ Summary of Medical Social Workers' duties

▶ Making sure the Discharge Plan serves the patient

▶ Unadvertised problems with hospital recoveries

▶ Discharge Plan Worksheet

"EMTs had to rush Dad to the hospital," Nancy blurted over the phone to her brother, Neal. "But he's OK for now, apparently."

"OK? We have to go see him right now!" Neal fired right back even though he lived on the other coast from their father. "How could I even break away from here until next week?"

"Same here, and then there's the kids."

"What does 'OK' mean? What happened?"

"They're running tests and don't seem to know, but his diabetes has gotten bad. So, he could have stroked. I did talk to a social worker there and with his nurse. I felt like he's in good hands. And he has time."

"So I'll go next week."

"Perfect, and again, the social worker sounded like an angel. She's there with Dad now, talking with him. She says he's confused about what happened to him. She's setting up a video chat so we can see him, as soon as he's able …"

—— 🏠 ——

When people think of social workers, they think of big-hearted people out there in the community helping families. And that's accurate. At the same time, some of the best social healing work is being done by Medical Social Workers.

You will find them on the front lines in hospitals, assisted living facilities, rehab centers, managed care organizations, and in hospice care. They focus primarily on supporting patients and their families in healthcare settings by coordinating patients' care with the larger medical team.

In that sense, Medical Social Workers are part of an interdisciplinary team of healthcare professionals who work together to help patients across the entire healthcare continuum.

Medical Social Workers lend their talents to the nonmedical aspects of patient care. This includes helping patients and families navigate the medical system, monitoring patients' and family members' mental and emotional health along the way, and providing upfront counseling and therapy when needed.

By bringing a patient's mental, emotional, familial, and social concerns into their treatment plan, Medical Social Workers ensure a more holistic, compassionate, and efficient level of care that improves health outcomes.

I know as well as anyone that a life-threatening disease or severe injury can be confusing, traumatic, and deeply stressful—all of those things—for patients and their loved ones. Medical Social Workers can step right to the bedside. They can talk through the medical diagnosis with the patient. This can help so much in turning medical speak into understandable terms, so the patient knows what to expect of the medical emergency they are involved in.

For the Medical Social Worker, their work environment is actually a very stressful place. It's fast paced, with constant pressures on them. Yet the ones I've talked to all say the same thing. The relationships they build up with patients, families, and the medical teams they work with, combined with the knowledge that they are truly helping individuals, make their work truly rewarding.

Summary of Medical Social Workers' duties and responsibilities

- ☐ Coordinate patient care in collaboration with the medical team.
- ☐ Communicate patient information to the health team.
- ☐ Keep an eye on the patient's and family's mental and emotional health.
- ☐ Provide counseling or psychotherapy to patients and families.
- ☐ Assess the family's financial circumstances and ability to pay for caregiving.

☐ Connect patients and families with outside medical and non-medical resources.

Making sure the Discharge Plan serves the patient

When being discharged from the hospital, a Medical Social Worker should be there to ensure that the patient will be properly cared for in the days and months ahead.

This process is called a Discharge Plan, and the goal is to determine the kind of living situation that'll be best after leaving the hospital. Discharge Plans can help prevent future hospital readmissions by ensuring the move is done with a full understanding of the best living situation for the patient.

This Discharge Plan should lay out where the patient will go next, what kind of care will be needed, and who will provide that care.

A Medical Social Worker can be very helpful at this stage because some hospitals have good protocols in place for evaluating the needs of discharged patients, but others do not. Having an ally there at discharge can make all the difference in the recovery and transition period.

Of course, the default position is always for patients to return to their current house, if possible. That means looking at the house and judging how suitable it is for in-and-out caregivers, any medical equipment that needs to be moved in, and any major alterations that need to be made to the house to ensure safety.

Often this evaluation will raise a difficult but important question. Namely, is the patient going to thrive best in the old home as it must be modified, or should an alternative living situation be discussed?

The Medical Social Worker will have the understanding to talk about this thoughtfully and recommend alternative living arrangements if that becomes an imperative. As well, the Medical Social Worker can help arrange referrals for future caregiving, including referrals to physicians, home health, skilled nursing facilities, memory care, and hospice.

If paying for assisted living will be a problem, sometimes the Medical Social Worker can help arrange funding through Medicaid and other programs. If the patient is short on funds or depends on assistance to pay for a living community, the social worker is often tasked with making that happen.

The Medical Social Worker will also be available to assist when a patient is checking out of the hospital and can even help craft a Discharge Plan. Here's a worksheet to guide you in working with your Medical Social Worker to craft a thoughtful Discharge Plan.

Discharge Plan worksheet[18]

To make the transition from the hospital to the most appropriate living situation, talk with hospital staff and your Medical Social Worker about key next steps.

- *Are the procedure results understood?* All treatments and test results, as well as follow-up appointments, should be thoroughly explained to the patient and family, though this is often not done. If test results are not available at discharge, let the patient and family know when they will be ready, since decisions often need to be made based on that information to come.

- *Is the house ready?* Is it built to accommodate any changes in the patient's health? Do modifications need to be made before it is ready and safe?
- *What support will be needed?* Who in the family can be there to help with physical needs given the new limitations? What kinds of modified meal plans might be necessary? Which activities can now be done, and which must be avoided?
- *What medications are prescribed?* Does the patient fully understand the purpose of each medicine on the medication list? How much to take, how to take it, and potential side effects? If the patient will be alone, this can obviously become a safety issue and needs to be taken very seriously.

With a caring and attentive Medical Social Worker guiding you through the process, you can be assured that the hospital stay and transition into the next stage of life will go as well as possible. Also helpful during this time are the Hospital Ombuds, which we'll talk about next.

9

Hospital Ombuds

HIGHLIGHTS

▶ Ombuds duties and responsibilities

▶ Helping while in the hospital

▶ Helping when leaving the hospital

"Fun fact," the sweet woman at Jilly's bedside said, "the word Ombudsman comes to us from Sweden and basically means 'representative.' Sweden was the first to appoint these Ombuds back in 1809 to be 'representatives of the individual' and to do their work based on four principles: confidentiality, informality, impartiality, and independence.[19] And so I am here for you, just you, as you take your next steps out of this hospital."

"Thank you so much," Jilly said, "because after this hip and knee surgery, I'm not sure what I'll be able to do next."

Ombudsmen, Ombudspersons, Patient Relations representatives, Ombuds—my favorite—there're lots of names now being used for these volunteers who are available to patients *at no charge* under a program run by the federal Administration on Community Living.

There's a nationwide network of some 6,000 volunteers and 1,400 paid staff all certified to handle patient questions, complaints, and concerns about the many complexities and uncertainties of medical care.[20]

At the Cleveland Clinic, for instance, the Ombuds handle some 22,000 cases a year.[21] And Stephanie Bayer, Director of Patient Experience there, says that often patients "come to us so confused, and when they leave they are so pleased, they send thank-you notes." It is a wonderful service, and Ombuds play an important role for patients still in the hospital and when they leave as well.

Ombuds' duties and responsibilities

Ombuds play a unique and wide-ranging role in the hospital system. They can step in at the patient's request to help with all kinds of matters related to day-to-day care, health, and safety of the patient.

The patient is always in charge and can ask an Ombud for help in making well-informed decisions. That can mean aiming to attain the highest standard of care in the hospital, helping to navigate today's often complex healthcare system, and transitioning successfully back into a life of the patient's choosing.

Ombuds are especially helpful when a loving and attentive family needs help out of necessity. Maybe the family lives far away, has job commitments, or experiences other issues creating a gap in their ability to be there. Ombuds can fill that gap and provide impartial guidance and recommendations to the patient. This support can begin from the first steps into the hospital to the last steps in leaving and resuming life and can include the following:

HELPING WHILE IN THE HOSPITAL

☐ Acting as a point person for patients and family members to discuss concerns about the medical treatment being given

☐ Arranging meetings with relevant members of the medical team to talk about any treatment concerns

☐ Answering any number of questions from how to seek legal aid if needed to how to obtain the best Medicare benefits if needed

☐ Advocating on behalf of the patient when there are concerns about violations of rights or dignity, or about poor-quality care or physical or mental abuse, or improper transfers or discharges. In these worst-case situations, they have the patient's back and can help lower the stresses of hospital stays

☐ Summarizing a patient's medical history into a clear and concise chart to improve patient care and reduce the potential for medical error

HELPING WHEN LEAVING THE HOSPITAL

☐ Orchestrating the discharge from the hospital along with the medical team and social workers

☐ Helping to arrange for private-duty nurses and therapists

☐ Suggesting modifications that will be needed to the home. Or, if the home no longer works because of the medical condition, outlining the options for the next chapter in life

☐ Identifying the top continuing care retirement communities in the local area for a patient needing to move into assisted living

☐ Appealing to Medicare to gain admittance to a preferred assisted living community

As I noted in chapter 8, patients are sometimes discharged from the hospital too early and can wind up back in the hospital far too soon.[22] One in five patients is rehospitalized with a medical problem, the statistics show. Often it results from returning to their home and trying to resume life "as it was before."

Ombuds are familiar with these one in five numbers. Over time they will develop a strong gut feel, along with their own reading of the Discharge Plan, about how the senior will fare back in the house, and whether the family is well advised to think through the senior's new living situation.

Consider the Ombud an ally and sounding board in deciding next steps after a hospital stay.

☐ Could it be that a return to the old house is just buying time because staying there is now unlikely?

☐ Will it become necessary to sell the house just to be able to afford long-term care in a retirement home?

These are two key questions the hospital Ombud can help with. The Ombud can help find the right community to move into as well.

Families choosing to augment the services of an Ombud can also hire a private patient advocate. This is a service provider that performs a similar role and can get more involved in fighting for the patient's needs and concerns, since the senior or family is paying for these services. These advocates have often been in the same situation. They know how the system works and can become a valuable ally, as well.

This completes our survey of the professionals who can help with the "move in," so let's look at your options for paying for the care a loved one may need.

10

Paying for the Care You Deserve

HIGHLIGHTS

▶ Applying for Medicaid assistance

▶ Taking out the right insurance policy

▶ Applying for veterans benefits

▶ Grabbing tax breaks

▶ Falling back on a reverse mortgage

▶ Finding more affordable assisted living

▶ Selling the home at the right time

David had signed up for a long-term care policy in his fifties when some health issues began nagging at him. His daughter, Jean, had helped him with all the paperwork. But when visiting her dad recently, she spied a cancellation notice among the clutter on his kitchen counter. He hadn't been paying his premiums.

"Dad, why aren't you keeping this policy active?"

"Because I turned sixty-five, dear, and won't need it anymore what with Medicare and my California teacher's pension."

"Dad, neither of those cover long-term care!"

Jean hopped on the phone to the insurance company and refused to get off the phone until the policy was reinstated. And a fortunate thing, because not long after David fell and tumbled down the stairs. He spent weeks in the hospital with more broken bones than he could count. When finally released, he wasn't returning home.

Jean moved him into an assisted living facility near to her. The long-term care policy covered most of the costs. And she wasn't going to have to sell the house right away to pay for David's care.

"We got lucky, Dad. Most don't."

Many seniors do, in fact, believe that Medicare or Medicaid will take care of their long-term care needs. But that couldn't be further from the reality they'll face. Medicare doesn't cover anything. And Medicaid can help but only for seniors with few assets and a low household income. Each state administers this program differently, but the basics don't vary.

Statistically, seven in ten older Americans will need some type of long-term care at one point, according to the US Administration on Aging.[23] And to pay for it, these people will depend on a combination of insurance or annuities, personal savings or investments, income from Social Security or pension benefits, reverse mortgage strategies, or the proceeds from selling their home.

We'll look at these financing strategies and options to help make the care you need obtainable.

Right from the start, some options will be limited. That's because several strategies for long-term funding require decades of planning and foresight. As in, starting in your forties. But let's look at all the options...

Applying for Medicaid assistance

Medicaid does help cover the costs of assisted living in some states. You have to qualify both medically and financially and go into a Medicaid-approved facility.

To qualify for Medicaid assistance, you need to be considered impoverished. While it varies by state, in 2023, a senior needed to show income of less than $2,472 a month with less than $2,000 in assets to qualify.[24]

Another thing about Medicaid that surprises people: Medicaid will offer assistance, but they do want to be paid back. If you take Medicaid funds and try to hold on to your house or other valuable assets to leave behind to the children, it won't happen. Medicaid will come after your estate when you pass to get repaid. The house you tried to leave to your children will have to be sold (in most states) to pay back Medicaid, and your children won't get much, if anything.

If Medicaid is your best funding choice, get proactive. Retain an attorney to talk about strategies for shielding the assets you want to pass on. Those protections must be in place long before going on Medicaid because they look back at your finances for five years in determining eligibility. They do this to prevent applicants from giving away assets in order to appear poor. Then if Medicaid finds that their rules have been violated, they will penalize you. During the penalty, you cannot receive benefits even if you otherwise qualify.

Since Medicaid is limited, people usually look to other funding resources.

Taking out the right insurance policy

Long-term care insurance policies are popular funding solutions and come in an assortment of prices, policy types, and coverage amounts. The older you are when you buy the policy, of course, the higher the premiums. If your health is poor, you may not qualify for insurance or face hefty premiums. Generally the coverage will kick in when you can no longer perform at least two tasks of daily living, such as bathing and dressing.

The cost of long-term care insurance depends on factors such as your age, gender, preexisting health conditions, and the benefits you choose. This insurance can easily become intolerably expensive where you're spending more for the premiums than you would for the care. I know people whose premiums doubled when they approached retirement age. It was no longer affordable to them even after paying into it for years. One friend of mine decided to invest her money instead in hopes of generating enough profits to pay for care.

And indeed, a Boston College study found that one in three people who buy long-term insurance policies at age sixty-five or older will have their coverage lapse before the insurance company pays out a nickel.[25]

All that said, if you obtain a policy early enough and can afford to make regular payments, it's a good funding option.

If you have a life insurance policy (whole or universal), you can tap the policy's built-up cash value. If you merely borrow from the policy on the premiums you've paid in (known as the cost basis), you pay no tax. But if you cash out entirely, you pay income tax on the policy's total value less the cost basis. That's why financial advisors often recommend withdrawing on your cost basis and borrowing any other funds you may need if that's an option.

A deferred long-term care annuity is another strategy. It is available to people up to age eighty-five. It's a way to pay in premiums, and the insurance company later pays out monthly income for a preset period of time. So it's a fund for long-term care expenses. The annuity won't usually cover all of your long-term care, but it can supplement. And if these funds are not used to pay for care, they will pass on to your heirs—which is a benefit.

There are also new hybrid products that combine life insurance with a long-term care rider. The idea is that policy benefits will be paid out either in life insurance or in long-term care.

Each of these policy options can and should be discussed with an insurance agent or elder care attorney.

Applying for veterans benefits

The Veterans Administration helps both veterans and their widowed spouses in need with what's known as Aid and Attendance payments of up to $2,100 a month.[26]

Veterans and surviving spouses who have documented physical or mental restrictions or disabilities, or who need help with everyday activities such as dressing, bathing, feeding, and the like, can qualify for assisted living help.

For more information visit:

- benefits.va.gov/pension
- va.gov/pension

Acquiring tax breaks

There are a couple of tax moves that appreciably change the financial picture when long-term care costs are looming.

If you are an adult child helping a parent afford long-term care, you may wish to claim a parent as a dependent on your federal tax return. This can be done even if you do not live together. If you are paying more than half of your parent's support, and their gross income is less than $4,400 a year (excluding tax-exempt income and Social Security benefits), you may be eligible for a dependent care tax credit.[27]

For more information visit:

- irs.gov/forms-pubs/about-publication-503

As well, if you are covering more than 50 percent of a parent's assisted living costs, you can deduct these costs from your taxes when they exceed 10 percent of your adjusted gross income.[28]

To maximize this deduction, pay for assisted living with taxable distributions from a retirement account. Though there's a 10 percent limit, an assisted living bill of $70,000 a year, for example, is going to result in a sizable tax break for most people.[29]

A good tax professional can help with these strategies.

Falling back on a reverse mortgage

If the goal is to remain in your current home, there is a tool that financial advisors call "the last resort." It's a reverse mortgage, and it will not only provide the funds needed but also strictly limit your options and even create serious problems down the road.

With a reverse mortgage, you basically take out a big loan on your home's equity. You can take the loan in a lump sum or choose to draw down the money when you need it. You can draw down a maximum of 74 percent of your home's value, depending on your age.[30]

Reverse mortgages are rather expensive, with thousands of dollars in closing costs, and the government takes a cut that can run as high as 2.5 percent of the loan value.[31]

These loans do not have to be paid back until you leave the house or pass away. But you must continue paying all insurances, property taxes, and upkeep expenses. Since these expenses can add up, they can quickly draw down the entire loan. If that happens, there may be no money left for other expenses. And at that point, the option of moving into an assisted living facility is no longer viable.

Nonetheless, this reverse mortgage is worth discussing with your financial advisor or an elder care attorney.

Finding more affordable assisted living

Some living communities are strictly private pay with no wiggle room on pricing or discount deals and have long waiting lists at the prices they charge. But others will be more accommodating. Here are some things to look for to save money:

FLEXIBLE PRICING

If a community offers all-inclusive pricing, that means their price includes all the services they offer. But if tiered pricing is offered, then less costly levels of care can be obtained, such as limiting the number of hours of care a resident receives. Basically, paying only for services desired.

However, in choosing a pricing tier that covers less, be careful. Some communities lock in their fee structures and may not change them later when circumstances require it.

OPEN BEDS

If a community experiences a drop in residents and is eager to maintain full capacity, you may be able to negotiate reduced rates, or even a month free.

LOWER-COST ROOMS

Community rooms are often priced by size and location. If a resident is comfortable in a studio apartment, or can be further away from the dining room, there are savings to be had. Or if residents can share a one-bedroom unit, basically turning the living room into a bedroom, they may be able to save up to 50 percent at some facilities.

For help in obtaining these lower prices or discount availability, a Senior Placement Agent and elder care attorney can both be valuable allies.

Selling the home at the right time

Ultimately, the decision on funding long-term care is driven by the cost of that care and the senior's assets. The cost of long-term care in an assisted living facility is averaging $54,000 a year, with nursing homes running to $106,000 a year.[32] If that kind of cash can be pulled out of a combination of Medicaid payments, veterans benefits, and insurance policies, then those are good options.

But they are rarely enough.

For most of us, the equity we have in our homes will become the best source of cash and most cost-effective option for paying for long-term care needs.

For this reason, we'll next talk about the best ways to maximize the value of a current house to pay for the level of care that may be needed. In Part III, we'll lay out a total home downsizing solution.

Introducing Home Downsizing Solutions

Turning Downsizing into a Delight (Almost!)

11

HIGHLIGHTS

- ▶ You'll be downsizing the right way
- ▶ Your stuff will all find the right home
- ▶ Your house will be ready to sell
- ▶ You'll find the best new home
- ▶ Moving out will go smoothly for you
- ▶ The house will sell successfully

Let's just say it. Downsizing can be a rocky road. It can quickly become an overwhelming experience whether you're facing it alone or the family is involved. Which is why several years ago, I decided that there had to be a simpler, easier, saner approach to it all.

There had to be a way to chart a straight line through all the stress of downsizing to the success of downsizing.

With more than twenty-five years in the property business, I've seen every kind of home selling situation in every kind of market. Through it all, I've learned a thing or two about drawing that straight line from the *start* of downsizing onto the *finish* so that it can go as smoothly as possible. So I took all this learning and simplified it down to one crisp idea.

And it, very simply, is that your downsizing will go better if you are left in control of all the decisions but have help at your beck and call, from A to Z in the process, there for you only when you need it.

That help, if you need it, is the concierge service we talked about in the beginning of this book. It's a service made available on a complimentary basis—just as a hotel concierge is. Offered to you by the same professionals you may be working with on your downsizing journey. This puts everyone on the same page, in service of your best interests.

That service I'm talking about is called *Home Downsizing Solutions concierge services.*

It's a service designed to help you with every aspect of transitioning to your new home and moving into your next season in life.

In fact, there are six steps in these concierge services. You can step through them over six months, six weeks, or even six days if you need to move quickly. Your own schedule dictates the time it takes to complete the downsizing transition.

Now let's be clear. You may be able to complete all these downsizing steps on your own or complete many of them anyway. But if at any point you need concierge assistance at your side, you can have it.

So let's jump into the six steps to a successful downsizing and the journey ahead.

1. You'll be downsizing the right way

BEGIN WITH A GIFT TO YOURSELF

Whether your downsizing will take six months, six weeks, or six days, let it begin with a gift to yourself: the gift of time. Pause to reflect on all the memories and moments this house has given you, and draw strength for the labors ahead.

If there's a single reason for putting off downsizing, even when it has to happen, it is stuff. Right? All of the possessions we've accumulated over time and the thought of dealing with all of it. The "dealing with it" can be stressful—physically, emotionally, all the *-allys*! But only if we allow ourselves to think about it that way.

If instead we wave our magic wand and look at the whole process as a straight path to a destination ahead, a golden mean of downsizing, we can just toe that line. One step after another. Along the golden mean. So take a breath and take the time to appreciate all that has brought you to this moment. It's a gift we can all use and yours to take now!

But don't just take it. Take it in an escape or retreat room—one place in the house where you can step back in the weeks and months ahead and relax, totally relax, away from the checklists and decisions and calls to be made. Younger folks might call it a safe place. Call it what you like, just let it be a place to recharge and relax as things move forward.

VALUE OF BRINGING IN A SENIOR MOVE MANAGER

With this guide in hand, you will be able to handle each decision as it comes up. But you may still want help at hand. A Senior Move Manager (as discussed in chapter 3) can be brought in to help with the key things.

These professionals specialize in the first two concierge services—helping you decide what you will be able to take with you and what you won't, packing up everything on moving day and then unpacking in your new home.

Whether you use this professional or not, you'll also want to involve as many friends and family as you can. Get everyone involved and divide up the workload.

INVENTORY YOUR BELONGINGS

Start by making a list of things in the house. Just a list, nothing more yet. There will be time later to decide what happens to all these belongings. For now, you just want a full inventory, whether hand-written on a legal pad or entered into a spreadsheet. Works either way.

In doing this you'll surely discover how much stuff you actually have. It may be an eye-opener!

If you are an adult child inventorying a parent's house, this can get taxing. Preparing to get rid of your own stuff is one thing, but when there's family involved, it can be quite another. It's not the things themselves; it's the memories that go along with them.

I still recall when my mom passed. My siblings and I came in and went through all the items in the house. Some dated back to when we were kids, and we got pretty choked up. Through the tears and laughter, it was hard enough sorting through it all much less giving ourselves permission to throw anything away. But it was the tears and laughter that remain with us today, honoring our parents' love.

Take photos of everything in every room. You want photos of your stuff, but mostly you want a record of how you've set up your furnishings. Your next home will have different dimensions. But you can use your old layout to inform your new layout and transfer over your furnishings in a style and motif that please you.

Also be sure to take photos of all your electronic products from the rear view—to make sure all the wires and cords are easily put back in place where they belong.

ASSESS THE VALUABLE STUFF

Early in your sorting, your eye will naturally turn to the more valuable items. Decide if any of them are valuable enough to go out and have an appraisal done.

Most people's collections, however prized by the owner, have only limited value in the market. But you could just as easily find hidden treasure in those collections or in the dusty boxes in the attic.

An impartial appraiser, or an estate sale or auction company, can help you here.

Also be thinking ahead about how much space you expect to have in the new home and how much of the collections or prized memorabilia will fit into the new space.

START THINKING ABOUT THE "BIG ITEMS"

Certainly one of the big challenges of downsizing is deciding on the "big" pieces and whether they'll fit in the new home. A smaller home, or assisted living community, will put some hard limits on how much furniture and larger items you want to move with you.

You may find that your most favorite furniture won't fit in your new space. How to handle this? One way is to change how you think about it. Instead of focusing on what you're eliminating, decide what you can't live without. That's what you keep!

Once you know the square footage of your new home, you can make final decisions on what you'll be able to bring along. You can then sell, donate, or dispose of those items (we'll get to that shortly).

In thinking it through, it helps to draw up a floor plan of the current house and lay out the furniture where it currently sits. The photos you've taken will help in filling out this floor plan and for later keeping an accurate inventory of all you have.

Think about the major appliances—the refrigerator, freezer, stove and oven, and washer and dryer sets. Will you need to move these heavy appliances, or are they handled in the new home or community?

Will you need your car in your new neighborhood, or will you be walking more and using a community's transportation services?

While your mind is still on the big items, it's a good time to make sure your budget is big enough to handle all these big items. So next …

FIGURE OUT YOUR BUDGET

Downsizing a home usually means downsizing costs as well. A smaller home lowers the mortgage or rent payment, property taxes, insurance, utilities, and the like. This is the good news of downsizing, as long as you keep good tabs on it all.

A written budget is always a good idea, done in three parts:

1. Outline your current monthly expenses related to the house and other costs of living.

2. Figure out what your finances will look like after you move to the extent of your knowledge. Some costs will not change much.

3. Write out a list of onetime moving out costs (such as repairing the house for sale, the moving company, moving insurance, equipment rentals, packing supplies, etc.).

The difference between budget 1 and 2 will, of course, be the savings you realize from moving less the onetime costs in 3. Keeping these numbers in mind will also help you make some decisions about which big furniture or appliances should come with you and which should be replaced in the new home.

These figures are going to change over time, but they will help you plan and adjust things as you go. By way of illustration, many home sellers will rent a storage unit and move items there until they figure out if they really want or need those items. This brings on the additional expense of moving the items twice perhaps, as well as the cost of the storage unit. After these extra costs, often the items aren't needed anymore and will never be used again. So think about this now.

2. Your stuff will all find the right home

LET THE SORTING BEGIN

There are as many sorting strategies as there are organizing professionals eager to help with this critical task. The most popular is the four-pile sorting system and for good reason. It makes some hard decisions easier (as long as you stick with it).

To work this system, plan on creating four piles—each in a different spot in the house. Toss (gently!) things into the pile based on your quick decision about the item. (You can change your mind later, so don't think about it too hard.)

1. *Giveaway.* Items given to friends and family who will value them.
2. *Donate.* It's a wonderful feeling to be able to give useful items to charities that accept donations.
3. *Sell.* A lot of stuff can be sold in a lot of ways, and that can raise extra funds to pay for the move.
4. *Dump.* Some items were not meant to be recycled or reused and should rightly be scheduled for a dump run.

Some people add a fifth pile: *Can't decide!* I'll leave that to you, though I don't recommend it. Our goal in taking the stress out of downsizing is to take out as much uncertainty as possible, and putting off decisions only adds uncertainty.

But there's nothing wrong with postponing decisions about items you're on the fence about. Enjoy thinking about the memories associated with special belongings. It's usually the memories that have good hold on us, not the items themselves. And in so doing, a decision will present itself.

So begin sorting! As for how to approach it all, it's a good idea to ...

TAKE A FIRST PASS AT EVERYTHING

In working with more than a thousand people downsizing their houses, as well as with the Senior Move Managers helping them, I've discovered that it's usually best to begin the sorting in the small or unused spaces.

One, it's just easier because of the small volume. And two, a lot of "junk" can accumulate in the hall closets, linen closets, junk drawers, attics and crawl spaces, corners of the basement, outdoor sheds, and garages. These can be tackled in a couple of afternoons, and you can see progress being made.

With the easy stuff done, next expand into the main rooms of the house for things to toss into one of the four (or five!) piles.

Make a first pass at your clothes and shoes, telling yourself that you'll get rid of items you haven't worn in (two, five, seven, ?) years.

Move next into the kitchen. This room is full of appliances and cookware that you use often. These items may feel more important to you than you at first think (because you've used them so often). So approach it with the strategy I outlined earlier. Don't think about what you have to get rid of; think about what you don't want to live without, and keep only those items.

Collect all your cleaning products in one place. Try to use them up and not buy more before the move.

At one point you'll run smack dab into the Wall of Nostalgia. It's real! There's the macaroni art project, the sugar-cube pyramid from middle school, baskets full of half-used art supplies. Sorting through these and deciding what stays with you and what gets left behind can be agonizing. So let it be exactly that, because it's also a memory you can take with you—the most valuable of things you'll take with you.

In this first pass, you'll want to gather up all your important documents and store them in a safe place. Do this with close family or an elder lawyer at your side.

Go ahead and reduce your collection of books, DVDs, and CDs to a bare minimum. This will be an easy early win.

Gather up all the photo albums, recipe books, and other written items you may not have room for in your new home and take them to a service to digitize them. Or do it yourself, since it's so easy now. That way your family can always have a digital copy of your family memories to hold onto.

GET RID OF DUPLICATES

As you go through your things, you may find that you have two or three of some items. Certainly more than you need. An easy way to downsize is to eliminate these duplicate items. Cast off that second wool jacket, or that third serving dish, to keep only the items you really need.

This same thinking applies to your collections. The new home may not have space for your prized snow globe collection or the pickleball trophies. Letting go of these cherished objects can be difficult, so select your favorites and take photos of the rest, for memory's sake.

If you choose to keep just your best artwork, photographs, and keepsakes and discard the rest, you'll have a representation of these valuables, which can keep their memories close to your heart.

DECIDE ON AN ESTATE SALE OR AUCTION

In going through the possessions you won't be taking with you, or if you are going through a parent's home and liquidating the estate, you may find items worth nearly $10,000 or more. It then makes sense to contact an estate sale or auction company. Their job will be to find new homes for these items and generate the highest cash proceeds for you. (We talked in detail about estate sales and auction houses in chapter 5.)

GIVE ITEMS TO CHARITY

Giving items to charity can be a wonderful feeling. At *Home Downsizing Solutions* we have helped many seniors get rid of a lifetime of belongings when they downsize.

We know that it can be difficult for families to discard more valuable belongings. So we try to ease the pain by helping to find new homes for these belongings rather than tossing them out.

Perhaps some perfectly good suits and dresses can go to charities that help low-income individuals look better in job interviews. Or like-new mattresses, linens, and housewares can go to organizations that help the homeless get back on their feet again.

These are good things we can do.

SELL THE UNWANTED AND UNNEEDED

Soon, your four piles will be stacked high and it will be time to:

☐ Hold a yard sale.
☐ Give items to charity.
☐ Place items in consignment or pawn shops.
☐ Try to sell them online.

Getting even a little cash for your smaller items is much better than simply throwing them in the trash.

At this point, your possessions are all present and accounted for. You know what you're going to do with all of them, and you have already begun emptying the house. You will want to schedule a junk removal company to come in and clear out anything you won't be selling or taking with you.

Now it's time to turn to the house itself.

3. Your house will be ready to sell

UNDERSTANDING THE BUYERS

To prepare the house for sale, first take a good look at the house. Not as the homeowner you are but through the fresh eyes of a potential buyer.

If you've lived in your house for a decade or longer, and haven't performed any improvements, then buyers will immediately see any dated aspects to your house. Just because the house has been fine for you, it doesn't mean it will be fine for most homebuyers.

Over the twenty-five-plus years in real estate, I've heard hundreds of homeowners make comments similar to those listed next. Tell me if you think these comments are true or false.

WHAT SELLERS OFTEN SAY	TRUE	FALSE
If I update the house, the new buyer will probably change it anyway.	☐	☐
I most likely won't update it the way someone else would want.	☐	☐
The buyer is not buying a new house; this house is fine the way it is.	☐	☐
If I put more money in the house, I won't get it back out when I sell.	☐	☐

We're about to see that all four of these comments could be either true or false—depending on the situation. And the problem is, there's no way to know ahead of time whether they'll be true or false.

What we do know is that most people who go home shopping are looking at houses one after another, so they lose track of details and soon begin jumping to conclusions very quickly. They'll come away with an impression oftentimes and stick with it.

These home shoppers do not see the house as you've seen it over the years, growing to appreciate all that is good or ignoring all that's not so good about it.

If they don't like the way the house feels, even if they can't explain why, they'll simply go onto the next house. It is accepted wisdom that new paint and floor coverings can make a big difference in how a home presents. But many buyers find themselves focusing on what's *not* finished, *not* updated. That's because most buyers want to buy a house, move in, unpack, and live there. Period.

Since some home shoppers are also looking at a number of *brand-new* homes in their search, they are seeing homes with new paint, new floor coverings, new kitchens, and bathrooms with granite. Then, even without knowing it, they'll expect any house they see to have these high-end updates. You know this isn't logical, but who ever accused humans of being logical?

Then there's all of the home improvement shows on TV these days. Those shows turn scrap houses into high-end show homes, only increasing the expectations of your potential buyer. So as a seller, you need to cater to these expectations.

WALKING THE HOUSE

It's now time to walk the house. Do it with a second set of eyes at your side, ideally. A realtor can be valuable at this step, but a cautionary note here: most realtors will ultimately be focused on one thing—getting the listing. This can and all too often does cloud their judgment about what should be done, or not done, to the house to prepare it to sell. Later a realtor can become more valuable, but at this point:

- A Senior Move Manager is still helpful, because they work for you and their interests closely align with yours.
- A *Home Downsizing Solutions* consultant can also help you look at all your options for preparing the house for sale.

In walking the house, go through every room, open every closet and cabinet, and try to see it all with fresh eyes as a potential buyer would see it.

You want the house to appear spacious, clean, and well cared for as possible. You want buyers to be able to envision their own things in this home and feel there is plenty of storage space for them to fill with their own stuff.

You're going to be having strangers walking through your home soon, so as you walk through, make double sure that you have secured small valuables, firearms, and important papers.

You'll also need to remove your personal photos and items on display. Buyers who see these may feel that you really don't want to sell. That, and they'll have a more difficult time picturing themselves in the home and will instead think they're "trespassing" in someone else's space, making the sale more challenging.

In your walk-through, you may find that quite a few things need to be done to make the house show-ready. At this point, you have a choice ahead of you:

☐ You can bring in a home buying service to take your home as is (which we talk more about in chapter 13).

☐ You can begin updating and fixing up the house now to sell it yourself or with a realtor.

Let's look at the updates and how important they are.

THE SIMPLE HOUSE UPDATES

Handle the easier fixes.

- *Paint the house.* The biggest impact dollar-for-dollar comes from interior and possibly exterior painting. A lot of sellers worry about this. Is it best to (a) use colors you the seller like or (b) paint everything a light neutral color so that the buyer can see a blank canvas to work from? That's right, the answer is "b."

- *Install new floor coverings.* A common problem is outdated carpeting. As the seller, you may know that the carpet is fine with years of life left. However, if the carpet is more than five to seven years old, no matter the condition, most buyers are going to consider it outdated.

In today's market, hardwood floors are popular, but they need to be in excellent condition. If they are not, they should be refinished.

- *Make cosmetic updates.* Items such as older lighting fixtures and wall outlets may seem unimportant or trivial. But buyers can look at these items and conclude that the whole house is dated. These items are not too expensive to update (though the costs can add up when looking at the entire house, as you must).

Spend as much time on the exterior of the house as the interior. Make sure the landscaping grabs the eye, lending that all-important curb appeal to make a good first impression.

THE MAJOR FIXES TO THE HOUSE

Schedule any needed repairs or upgrades.

- *Renovate the kitchen.* If you're hoping to get a good price for the house, comparable to other houses sold in your area that look new, you need an updated kitchen. Some sellers push back on this, insisting that the buyer isn't buying a new house after all. While that is correct, the plain reality of the market is that buyers will be looking at other homes in your area that have sparkling new kitchens, and if yours doesn't, you'll need to lower your asking price to attract interested buyers.
- *Renovate the bathrooms, too.* Just as important as the kitchen are the bathrooms. Buyers are concerned with these, and, unfortunately, they are the most expensive to update. It is not unusual for nice bathrooms and kitchens to "sell" a house.
- *Update mechanical and structural systems.* Buyers will look at a worn roof or obvious cracks in the walls as a sign that expensive repairs may be looming. What's more, the buyer may not qualify for a loan or an insurance policy on the house if these major structural systems are not in good order.

A roof needs to have several more years of life in it. The heating and cooling systems, as well as the plumbing, need to be in good working order. A home inspection will shine the light of discovery on these items. But even before a buyer's home inspection occurs, it's important that you know how these major systems will impact the eventual sale price.

Generally speaking, the house has to be in good condition if you wish to receive a good price for it. This is the point where the selling process can get stressful, as I've often seen.

I've had sellers tell me, "We just met with two real estate agents who told us we need to do this, that, and these three other things to put the house on the market. But if we do all those things, we may just as well stay in our house."

Another thing I've heard often is, "I simply don't have the money to make all these repairs and updates."

Unfortunately, neither of these two scenarios—paying for tons of repairs and not having the money to pay for tons of repairs—solves the problem if you or a loved one needs to move into a smaller home or assisted living. You can't stay put, and you probably can't sell for a good price unless you do the fixes and updates. So what then?

Well, you can go look at the exteriors of houses that have sold recently in your area or possibly find interior pictures of them on real estate websites. Look at how they've been updated. Look over any online photos or floor plans that may exist on them. Get a better idea of how your house compares to them. This is called looking at "comps," and it tells you a lot. After doing this, try to decide what you can reasonably afford to do and still have a budget in place for your next chapter in life.

You can do this, but it's not likely to solve the problem you face. So I usually recommend that house sellers do either everything or nothing. That is, do all the updates and polishes the house needs or none.

Because again, when potential buyers walk into a house and see only some updates done, they right away begin wondering (even obsessing on!) whether there are other hidden "older house" problems that they might inherit if they buy the house.

So if the house definitely needs work, but that work will break the budget, then a traditional real estate listing may not be the best option. We'll talk about other options shortly.

HIRING A MOVING COMPANY

We're getting closer to the moving day, so it's time to schedule a moving company. A Senior Move Manager can be of invaluable help in selecting a trustworthy and dependable moving company as well as working out all the logistics. (We also talked in detail about these moving services in chapter 3.)

4. You'll find your best new home

ASSESSING YOUR NEXT HOME

Your next step is to finalize where you or your loved one is moving to. You most likely already have a pretty good idea or even know for certain—since the time frame on this decision can be longer.

If moving into a smaller home, be looking at homes, condos, and apartments in areas that interest you. It's time to talk with real estate agents, and look at online listings, to get ideas. Research as many homes in as many areas of interest to you as possible. Be thinking about what you want in a new space and how it will work for your lifestyle.

If moving into an apartment or a senior living community, be looking at your options—always keeping in mind that many communities have waiting lists and a decision needs to be made as early as possible on these. (Discussed in detail in chapter 4.)

PREPARING FOR THE NEW SPACE

If moving into a house, apartment, or senior living community, you'll want to get a copy of the floor plans of the new home or bring a tape measure and figure out the dimensions of each room. You can then figure out which of your furniture will fit and which won't. This is actually a critical step because you'll then know which of your larger objects you can bring with you and which need to be left behind. You can also begin planning out the decor and furnishings you want to add to your new home.

Now it's time to start packing. If you've put everything you're getting rid of into one of the four piles, all that's left is ready to be moved! Mark every item with a sticky note to direct the movers where to place the items in the new home.

5. Moving out will go smoothly for you

Now comes the big moving day! If you have been doing each of the steps faithfully, this fifth step should go smoothly. This is the time, working with your Senior Move Manager if you're choosing to, when you finalize all of the preparations and check everything off as complete.

- ☐ All donations have been dropped off or picked up.
- ☐ An estate sale or auction is scheduled or done.
- ☐ Home repairs, upgrades, and polishes are handled.
- ☐ Food in kitchen, pantry, and freezer are drawn down.
- ☐ A junk removal company is scheduled to take away any remaining items.

6. The house will sell successfully

In this sixth and final stage, the house sells successfully and you move on to your next chapter in life. Getting this sale right is so important; we'll focus on it in the next two chapters.

Summary of the six levels

We've now stepped through the six levels of downsizing and how *Home Downsizing Solutions* concierge services can help at every step—actually making the whole process a delight (almost!).

I'm providing this complimentary concierge service to seniors and their families because (a) I know the downsizing process is rarely an easy one and (b) I want to help make it as smooth as possible.

I know that downsizing is not just decluttering and moving—hard enough on its own. It's a really big life decision that requires an equally big solution, ideally one that is all coordinated and coming together in one place. A one-stop concierge coordinating it all just makes sense for everyone involved.

If all the professionals involved are coordinated into a single downsizing plan, the plan is going to go smoother, right? So *Home Downsizing Solutions* brings together downsizing professionals you can trust and value in these areas:

- Senior Move Managers
- Auction Services
- Estate Sale and Auction Specialists
- Junk Removal Specialists
- Home Remodeling Contractors
- Moving Companies
- Senior Real Estate Specialists

- Home Buying Services
- Packing/Unpacking Services

If you could use any of the concierge assistance I've talked about here, from how to begin downsizing the right way on through to selling your old home successfully, contact us.

- *Call our office*: 855-291-5005
- *Visit our website*: HomeDownsizingSolutions.com
- *Scan this QR code* with your phone and begin a text conversation with our team

Home Downsizing Solutions professionals are also available to give complimentary talks to senior communities, civic groups, and churches to help ensure more successful downsizings for our friends and neighbors in the years ahead.

12

A Reality Check before Selling the House

HIGHLIGHTS

▶ Getting the house ready for sale

▶ Putting the house on the market

▶ Ups and downs of showing the house

▶ Closing costs/surprises for the seller

"So happy you're finally home!" Daniel called out to Lori as she came back from a trip to her sister out in Minneapolis. "I've been in the lion's den all day here."

"I take it you didn't like any of the realtors?" Lori asked, bringing the wine bottle into the living room, leaving the glasses behind after hearing the nausea in Daniel's tone. They had lived in this musty, old Seattle house for about twenty years, they'd been unable to have kids, and now their doctor had advised moving to a desert community for their health's sake.

"Oh, the real estate people were likable enough," Daniel said, "but I don't think they heard a word of our concerns."

"Did you at least get an idea what we can make selling right now?"

"Not really."

"How about how long they think it'll take to sell, now that we have to move?"

"No, not that either."

"So we don't know how long we've got to keep this place spotless for their random showings?"

"Nope." Daniel tried to reply while tipping back the bottle, adding a new stain to the white carpet. Lori hopped up to grab the cleaning supplies, all part of the new "keep it spotless" routine. "Don't worry about the stain, Lori; we have bigger problems, I think."

"Like?"

"Like are we even going about this the right way? I'm not sure we are."

—— 🏠 ——

People buy and sell houses every day, and an entire industry has dedicated itself to creating a warm and fuzzy glow around the Real Estate Transaction. And yet that transaction can just as easily turn into a cold and sharp gloom if it hasn't been thought through completely.

So let's take a step back in this chapter and run a reality check on the whole process.

We have seen how all six steps in a downsizing can go perfectly well—if you're well prepared with good professionals at your side. But it's doubly important to spend some extra time on the challenges of that sixth step—the actual home selling step. That way you'll have all the information you need to make decisions that are in your best interests, with far less wine spilling!

Most of these challenges come as a result of the giant real estate industry's many ad campaigns and sales pitches aimed at convincing folks that the traditional sales approach is the best approach. When in truth, and I say this as a realtor myself, the traditional approach is only *usually* the best approach.

It isn't always, and let's look at why.

Getting the house ready for sale

As we discussed in the previous chapter, the first challenge you face becomes more obvious when you start getting the house ready for sale.

Do you know how a potential buyer is going to view your house through their eyes?

Do you have the funds to handle any updates or repairs that will be needed for the house to sell at a good price?

If you need to paint the exterior or interior, or put down new floor coverings, or tear out the kitchen and bathrooms and bring them up to today's standards of show quality, the house will be a mess during this time. Do you want to be living in the house while these updates and repairs are being done?

It also costs more—these days, often a lot more—to remodel and update a house than many people think. Estimates vary widely, of course, but costs can range from $40,000 to $300,000—depending on the project's extent and the square footage. The folks at Rocket

Mortgage put the national average cost at anywhere between $100,000 and $200,000 if major systems need updating.[33]

Beyond the expense of it all, do you want to find and interview contractors, get multiple quotes, and oversee all the work to ensure that it's done correctly?

If your expectations are to get "top dollar" when selling the house, the house better be nice and in better condition than the competition. If several years have passed since the last remodel or upgrade on the house, most buyers are going to come in with lowball offers.

If the real estate market happens to be hot when you sell, your troubles will be fewer, and you may get an offer you can live with. However, if the market has downturned, then buyers are going to shower you with discounted offers.

There are buyers who will put in an offer on a house that "needs work" because they'll welcome the challenge of doing the work themselves. But because most buyers lack the experience, the imagination, or the funds it takes to update a house, this option is usually off the table.

Putting the house on the market

At the outset, a real estate agent will typically be more optimistic than realistic when estimating what your house will sell for. The agent is trying to get your listing, after all!

If you decide to list, have the agent show you the market statistics for your area. Not just a few houses like yours but stats on all the homes that have been listed in your neighborhood. You want to know:

- What's your competition in nearby price ranges?
- What houses were put on the market but then didn't sell?

- Among those that sold, was the price over or under asking price?
- How long did it take those homes to sell?
- What was the condition of the houses that did sell?

You will also want to compare your house to different kinds of houses—such as a ranch house, two-story ranch house, split entry house, and the like. These may not be comps in the literal sense. What you're looking for is the condition they're in. That is, did the home sales that got "top price" have new kitchens and bathrooms with granite countertops, cabinets with slow-close drawers, and nice finishes like that? If they did, it will tell you the value of "nice" homes in your area and whether you really need to remodel or update to get a good asking price.

The ups and downs of showing the house

When it comes to living in a house while it is being shown by realtors, it can be a frustrating and difficult time. Especially in a down market, when the time that homes remain on the market tends to drag from weeks into many months. You need to be comfortable with, or at least tolerant of, the process.

As we've discussed, you'll have to keep the house in "show-ready" condition until it finally sells. You'll always have to "make yourself scarce" when on short notice the agent has a buyer in the neighborhood and wants to show your house.

This frustration can become outright annoying if you have to leave the house every time there's a showing, even at inconvenient times. Especially when a lot of these untimely intrusions come from buyers who are really not buyers, who could not even qualify for a loan, but who enjoy looking at other people's homes. Or they are posing as buyers to check out the house for valuables or medications they might be able to steal on the walk-through. It's a miserable thought, I know, but I've seen it happening more and more and you have to protect against it.

It's an even more miserable situation for seniors I've worked with who simply could not leave the house for health reasons (it happened a lot during the worst months of the COVID-19 pandemic). These seniors simply could not list their house the traditional way with all the showings it would require. So we took a nontraditional approach to a successful sale—one we'll talk more about shortly.

Not knowing when the house will sell

Often the biggest challenge home sellers face is not knowing when the house will sell so that they'll be able to move into their new home. It's hard to lock in a new home or senior living community when you don't know when you'll be free of the current house.

Or if you sell the house *faster* than anticipated, you may be forced to move twice. Once to a temporary hotel or similar arrangement and then again to where you actually planned to move in the first place.

There's also the flip side of that problem. You may be able to move into a new home right away, but then you could have a vacant house that you still need to take care of. You'll still need to, or should, keep the utilities on, keep it clean and in showing condition if it's still on the market, keep the insurance active—and those insurance premiums are much higher if the house is vacant and the risks for insurers increase. All of these can be manageable, since it's part of the Real Estate Transaction. But you have to be able to handle it. If that could be a problem, best consider alternatives to a traditional home sale.

Finding a buyer who can qualify for a loan

In recent years, more people have been purchasing homes for cash, and big institutional investors have added to those cash purchases. But a *Forbes* analysis found that still only a third of homes are paid for with cash.[34] That means most buyers will need to qualify for a loan, and that can be a difficult hurdle for many.

Then if that hurdle is cleared, the buyer's lender will require an appraisal of the house. The appraiser's job is to make sure there are no known deficiencies or defects with the house. The lender wants to know that they will not be making a loan on a house that would be a risky use of funds.

Another hurdle is the house inspection. Buyers naturally want to be sure they are not buying a house with defects, especially hidden ones. If the inspection comes back with a list of things to fix, and it usually does, this, in turn, becomes another negotiating opportunity for the buyer, another chance to drive the price down.

Again, this is all part of the traditional real estate transaction. You may find that it works to your advantage on your downsizing journey; you may find that it does not. And that's when you look at the alternatives.

Transaction costs/surprises for the seller

When the sale of the house finally closes, and the deal is done, there are still some worries that escape a lot of people's attention.

Namely, the costs of selling a house almost always add up to a lot more than you expect. These costs, known as transaction and closing costs, can include the real estate agent's commission, appraisal fees, pest inspection and whole house inspection costs, title service and settlement fees, title insurance, transfer tax, recording fees, and property taxes.

Most of these fees fall to the seller to pay out of the final home sale amount, while some can fall to the buyer to pay. But here's what happens. Often the buyers can only scrounge up enough money to cover the down payment they needed to secure a bank loan for the purchase. They simply cannot or as often choose not to cover the buyer's portion of the closing costs. Last minute, when the deal is all but done, they try to pawn those costs off on the seller. The seller doesn't have to pay them, but then the deal might fall through. So the seller often ponies up, wanting to be done with the deal and move on.

For this reason, the seller typically nets only 85–92 percent of the original asking price, assuming the house doesn't need updates or repairs. So the house that the real estate agent said could be sold for $300,000, as an example, could net only $255,000–$276,000. That's quite a haircut for taking the "traditional" approach to a home sale!

This is something I like to refer to as the Law of Gross versus Net.

Now with all of this said, remember that this is only a reality check.

As a real estate agent myself, I have a big belief in American private property and I value the hundreds of clients I've represented. But it is for this very reason that I developed the *Home Downsizing Solutions* solution. I want to provide a genuine service that solves problems instead of creating them. Doing that sometimes means selling houses the traditional way, sometimes not.

In the next chapter, we'll look at the alternatives for selling a house and moving onto the next season in life.

13

Options for Selling a House

HIGHLIGHTS

▶ Using a traditional real estate agent

▶ Selling the house yourself (FSBO)

▶ Working with a home buying company

There are basically three options for selling a house, and each has its own advantages—depending on your objectives. We'll look at each of these options, discussing the pros and cons of each of them, so that you can make the best decision for you.

Using a traditional real estate agent

The most common way to sell a house is by "listing" it with a real estate agent. This puts the house into the Multiple Listing Service (MLS), which pushes your house information onto a number of online sites for people to browse. This has the advantage of getting your house in front of thousands of other agents and their potential buyers.

This agent can lessen the stresses of selling by handling all the communications with buyers and their agents and all the paperwork involved in the transaction, lowering your need to be completely involved if that suits you.

Is the agent representing you well? In working with an agent, plan to manage their activities and make sure the wheels are turning toward a sale. Keep an eye on the following:

☐ Is the agent marketing your house to the fullest, or are they just sticking a sign in the yard, putting you on the MLS, and waiting for something to happen?

☐ Is the agent putting accurate information in the MLS? There is a lot of data to enter, and if the MLS database isn't properly populated, it can reduce the number of people who see your listing or invite the wrong people to view the house.

☐ Is the agent ensuring that your listing information is getting pushed to all of the online sites that it can be, for maximum exposure?

☐ Is the agent using photos of your house for the MLS listing that look great and show your house in the best light, or are they cutting corners that give the impression your house is in worse condition than it actually is? A good agent will use a professional photographer—to get the best pictures possible.

☐ Is the agent using all of the new technologies to create videos, virtual tours, and drone panorama shots that elegantly set your home in the neighborhood?

As we've talked about, listing with an agent means you will need to update the house so it is ready to show, open the house to prospective buyers, be comfortable with strangers, many who are looky-loos as they say, not at all serious but having fun walking through your house. All aspects of the listing process can go wonderfully, but it's largely out of your control for the period of sale.

How much time will it take? A house typically stays on the market from as little as thirty days as it was in summer 2022 to eighty-eight days as it was in January 2017.[35] So the average to expect is about sixty days on the market. From there, add in the time it takes to close a deal, which averages forty-three days. So you can figure on spending three and a half months in the selling process, not including the time needed to prepare the house for sale.[36]

Agent's optimism is a double-edged sword. Agents tend to be natural optimists, which makes them good at the job of selling. But if that optimism means they list your house at too high a price, it can burn you. A higher asking price sounds good at the outset, but if it's too high over market, the offers will not come in. Now the agent has to coax you into dropping your asking price, taking the price down to where it should have been in the first place. But now the house has been on the market too long, buyers see it as a "stale listing," and still no offers come in.

This kind of real estate sleight of hand happens far too often, but it can be avoided in one of two ways. The first, of course, is to work with a reputable agent. The second is to skip right past the traditional listing process and take an alternative approach. The first one available to you …

Selling the house yourself (FSBO)

This is the old do-it-yourself trick, and it's popular with people eager to save the 5–7 percent commission that gets paid to the agent(s) in a deal. It's called the "For Sale by Owner" option, or FSBO, and some 10 percent of all houses are sold in this manner. I think of FSBO as a kind of high wire act—it's wonderful to watch, as long as nothing goes wrong.

FSBO really means doing a lot of work. You'll want to make sure the house is priced properly for the market in your area. Research recent sales prices for comparable houses in your area. If a property is priced too high, it can sit ignored for months or even years, and you lose any negotiating leverage you have as a seller. Buyers know your position is weakened, that you have become more desperate to sell, and they will make offers even lower than the true market value of the house, assuming they will get it.

Spend the money to get a professional appraisal, to help you in setting the price at the right level. Visit open houses in the area to get a better idea of going prices.

GETTING THE HOUSE READY

As we have discussed in chapter 12, you'll need to make sure all the major systems in the house are in good working order. If you miss any problem, you can expect the buyer's inspector to catch it, and you'll have no choice but to repair or update the system before the closing.

Also make the home attractive. It should be clean and clutter-free. Surfaces should be freshly painted and carpets either very clean or new.

Be sure you are current on all your state's laws and regulations on fair housing, as well as all disclosures that must be made. Each state is different, with California requiring dozens of disclosures and Arkansas only a few to be in compliance. You do not want to risk a lawsuit for not disclosing some defect on your property.

There are also what's known as "Rules of Acceptance" that must be followed in your negotiations with the buyer. If you are working without an agent, it can be valuable to retain an attorney to make sure you do not run afoul of the law on this.

The biggest challenge in an FSBO is you still need to attract a buyer. If the market is on the upswing, this will not be hard. But if the market is cooling or even stuck in a downturn, buyers will be scarce.

Attracting a buyer will take money and time. So some of the cash you would have paid in agent's commissions will still leave your pocket. And figure on spending anywhere from thirty to one hundred hours on just the tasks of selling. So you should first set a value of your time before deciding if this approach is right for you.

HOW WILL YOU ATTRACT POTENTIAL BUYERS?

Old-fashioned methods still attract buyers. A sign in the yard with a flyer box is an obvious first step. Putting up flyers at work or in stores is also worth the effort.

There are also online services you can list on now, including Zillow, BuyOwner, ForSaleByOwner, and FSBO.net. For a relatively small fee, you can reach many thousands of house hunters on these services.

You can also now get listed in the MLS for a flat fee using a service such as Houzeo, though in some cases, using the MLS may require you to pay a buyer's agent commission.

A CAUTIONARY NOTE ABOUT SHOWINGS

Be careful, especially during an open house, on whom you allow to walk through the house. Most viewers will not be a worry, of course. But some will have less than pure motivations, and you need to screen and monitor them as best as possible (in this regard, selling the house yourself is no different from using an agent).

Next, most of your potential buyers will have an agent representing them. The buyer and agent know you are an FSBO and trying not to pay commissions. So the buyer will often ask you to pay their agent's half of the commissions. You can say no, but then it becomes a negotiation with you needing to make sure the buyer doesn't walk away.

Once you have an interested buyer, the next step is to determine if they really can buy the house. Few will be able to make the all-cash offer required for a quick close. Do they have the ability to obtain the loan they need? One of the most frustrating things to hear a buyer say is "I am preapproved," only to discover that the loan preapproval is conditional on a number of items the lender hasn't ticked off yet.

Depending on the type of loan the buyer is seeking, the lender may be ready to fund when the buyer is ready to sign. Or the lender may *actually* have given a conditional preapproval online or over the phone but now needs to see a number of documents to decide if the buyer actually qualifies for the loan.

Worth noting: This loan approval hassle can just as easily happen when working with an agent. If you opt to use an agent, be certain that the agent is authorized to communicate with the buyer's lender on the status of the loan.

Also as with the agent option, plan on the entire process taking about six months—from getting the house ready, through showing the house, to closing the sale. And when you do close, you'll want to hire a lawyer to draw up a sales contract and make sure everything is up to snuff.

So there is plenty of work in FSBO, and it's not right for every situation, but for those who have the time and interest in working hard to sell the house and save some money, this alternative can be a good one.

There's one more alternative.

Working with a home buying company

A total alternative for selling your house is to use a home buying company. This is a specialized company that is involved in real estate, just like a realtor; only they take it a step further. They can come in and swiftly take the property off your hands with minimum hassle.

Buy it from you directly, in short.

And it's the ideal solution for selling the house with the least stress of any option. That's its big selling point. But like working with an agent or doing it yourself, there are ups and downs to this approach.

The biggest downside, frankly, is the number of companies out there claiming to be legitimate "home buyers" when they are nothing of the sort. The internet is littered with outfits that will supposedly make cash offers for homes right over the phone—without even seeing the house.

Or companies that look up the address online, see the latest assessed value, divide it in half, and make that the offer.

Or companies that advertise on city bus benches or use boiler rooms full of cold callers trying to pressure people into selling right now.

Or companies that really are just hustlers out there, making cash offers and then retreating to the bank in hopes of securing a line of credit against the house in order to actually pay for it.

You can protect yourself from being stung in this type of situation in two ways:

1. Ask to see proof of funds up front—that will weed out the pretenders, usually.
2. Contact the title company of the buyer, and ask if the buyer is "real" and if they can actually do what they say they can.

Some home buyers will make a decent-enough offer on the house and then begin a long tortured process of nickeling and diming you down on repair costs, closing costs, extra fees, and so on. This very thing can also happen when using an agent, but you have more protections in place with an agent. In working with a home buyer, be prepared to hold the line on the minimum price you will accept. It may be worth it to you, because there are also many positives in working with a genuine home buying company.

WHAT MAKES HOME BUYING SERVICES SO POPULAR

HOME BUYING EXPERIENCES

I had planned to sell my house conventionally, but life situations changed quickly, and I didn't want to take the extra time to make repairs before listing on the MLS and waiting for a

> buyer to maybe come along. [Ben] came in, walked through the house, took notes and some pictures, and I had an offer with two options by the next day. ... I was given a month to move out and was told if I needed more time or less time, that was fine.
>
> **—Maggie Giamalvo**

Namely, you can sell your house quickly or when you want to. And you remain in control throughout the sale of your house, A to Z. You decide when to sell. You decide when to move. You can get a custom solution to address your biggest needs as a seller. This is one of the services my team and I provide through *Home Downsizing Solutions*.

Using our home buying service, your home sale can be concluded as soon as the title and closing company checks the title and prepares the closing paperwork.

We can buy your house as is and pay cash regardless of the house's condition or why you are selling it. There are times that we can also purchase all of the "stuff" in the house. These are usually situations where a person doesn't have enough stuff for an estate sale or auction.

We can assess your property's market value, make a fair cash offer, and close the sale in seven days or less, guaranteed. You make zero repairs or upgrades. Plus, you pay no realtor commissions or other selling expenses. We'll even pay up to 100 percent of the closing costs and assist you in moving into your new home.

All of the complicated steps in the selling process, prepping the house for sale, hiring a realtor, staging and showing the house, scheduling inspections, haggling with buyers, negotiating the best sale price possible, finally closing, and then waiting for funds to clear escrow—all of these are eliminated with our home buying service.

Instead you have a private one-on-one transaction.

You don't have to get involved with banks, lenders, agents, or home shoppers.

You simply schedule a quick walk-through and let us assess your property. We'll perform an inspection and check your area values, which can allow us to make one or more offers on the spot!

HOME BUYING EXPERIENCES

My sister died in December 2020. My brother and I live in a different state [and] knew that the best thing would be to sell the house as quickly as possible because we didn't want it to stay vacant. Ben Souchek had top quality people ... so efficient and professional and helped us through all the proceedings. Everyone was so kind, quickly returned our calls and answered our questions. The whole procedure flowed so flawlessly.

—Anne Schultz

If you accept our offer, the final step is to close the sale. A title transfer company can process the paperwork and close in only a few days without any seller closing costs. Those are 100 percent paid, for savings right away.

There are no commissions or fees to pay in selling your house this way, so all your money goes toward creating a comfortable retirement lifestyle for you or your loved one.

Since I specialize in senior transitions, I recognize that the *timing* of the house sale is critical. If the house sells but the new home is not ready to move into for whatever reason, that creates a problem.

In fact, this happened early in my career. A seller I was working with was on a waiting list for an apartment community. They knew they would be moving in the next thirty to ninety days but didn't know exactly when it would happen. But they did need to sell their house to afford the move and the new home. So I came up with a solution when none existed.

TO THINK ABOUT

What if you want to sell your home but don't have a new home lined up? That's a problem **Home Downsizing Solutions** can solve by buying your home but letting you stay in it for sixty days, ninety days, or even longer. So you have time to transition into a new home hassle-free.

I closed the sale on their house, giving them the peace of mind that the house was in fact sold. But I structured the deal so they could remain in the house until they were able to move. The house was sold, but they could stay in it for thirty days, sixty days, even ninety days, or longer if needed. So they could transition without any clock ticking away the hours of stress on whether they'd be able to move. It all worked beautifully.

So beautifully, my company has been doing that very thing ever since!

And the best part of this one-stop solution is that it carries through to the next stage, ensuring that the transition to a new home also goes smoothly.

For example, we allow our sellers to leave any last items they don't want to bother moving. They don't have to order a dumpster or a junk hauler to come in. They just take the things they want to keep, sell the things they want to sell, and leave the rest. No need to leave the house spotless like when selling to a traditional buyer. That's handled.

Summary comparisons

Ultimately, the best way to sell a house depends entirely on what you value most.

If you value a stress-free transaction, or one that is completed quickly and effortlessly no matter what's going on in the current real estate market, then the *Home Downsizing Solutions* option is the best one for you.

If you value getting every dollar out of your house that you can, then a traditional realtor may be the better option. And I say "may" because those extra dollars could shrink down fast once you factor in the repairs you'll be asked to make, getting and keeping the house in show-ready condition, realtor commissions, closing costs, and other selling expenses. Plus, the entire process could take three to twelve months. Do you want to wait that long to downsize?

So again, it comes down to what you value. Give thought to that as you look at this summary of your three options.

House Selling Options

	REALTOR	FSBO	HOME BUYER
Commissions or Fees	6%	0	0
Closing Costs	Up to 8%	Up to 8%	0
Appraisal Required	Yes	Yes	No
Showings	Yes	Yes	No
Repairs/Renovations	Yes	Yes	No
Average Selling Time	60-90 Days	6-12 Months	3-21 Days

As we've seen, downsizing is a great solution for easing the burden of a larger house and simplifying your life. The next choice—whether it is using a realtor, selling it yourself, or working with a home buyer—is now in your hands!

Let's talk more about that.

14

Finding the Right Real Estate Professional

QUESTIONS TO ASK

► Are you a legitimate home buyer?

► Are you going to look at my house?

► How did you come up with the offer?

► Do you provide multiple offers or solutions?

We discussed the different options for selling a house in the previous chapter, so now let's dig deeper into the most important details of finding the right real estate professional. The real estate professional can assure the best outcomes in this transition to a new chapter in life as they are the most involved in the downsizing move.

In a nutshell, the success or failure of selling a house and downsizing often depends on finding the right real estate professional.

So let's first handle a touchy subject. A lot of home sellers have family members or friends who are realtors, and they'll feel pressure to work with family and friends. But frankly, it is rarely a good idea. The family and friends may be highly talented, but they cannot serve as an impartial agent—because they have history and personal feelings, which can easily get in the way of securing the best deal, as we will see.

If you do want to use family and friends as agents, then be sure to do your due diligence on them just as you would for anybody you are considering (even tell them you're doing this to avoid any hurt feelings). Then your decision will be a better one.

Choosing the right agent in an ocean of them

There are now more than 1.5 million licensed realtors in the states, more of them than lawyers, doctors, or accountants.[37] Decades of booming housing prices and people looking for cushy jobs collecting commissions by showing houses ("OMG, that's so me!") have created a glut of agents. Finding the right one can make you feel like you're the kid, shovel in hand, standing outside the barn, looking in on piles of manure, thinking, "There must be a pony in here somewhere!" So how best to wade in and find the pony?

I always recommend finding an agent who has a Senior Real Estate Specialist (SRES) designation or at least has deep experience working with downsizing on a regular basis. These are the professionals who will become valuable resources when the challenges of a senior transition begin presenting themselves, and the agent's problem-solving skills are needed.

The best agents are what I term Total Solutions Agents™. These are agents that can not only list your house but also work with legitimate home buying companies, to provide multiple solutions to get your house sold.

> ## SENIOR EXPERIENCES
>
> Since my father moved to Arizona, suffers from health issues, and all us kids live out of state, we needed to get Dad's house sold quickly and efficiently. ... The conventional agent, understanding our circumstances, referred us to Ben Souchek. ... We appreciated Ben's professionalism, understanding, honesty, and fair offer. Sometimes, "as is" is definitely a good thing. So much weight off our shoulders .
>
> **—Betty Flores**

Any real estate agent you consider working with should be well-versed in the key value-adds of the job:

- *Informs you* about the different types of homes and living communities that best suit your needs going forward.
- *Arms you* with the questions to ask about each of the professionals who will be involved in the downsizing (basically, being on top of the information in this book).
- *Introduces you* to financial specialists knowledgeable in senior living options and best able to help you leverage the value you'll be getting in your next living arrangement.
- *Directs you* to legal assistance you may require in downsizing as well as estate or asset protection planning, as needed.

- *Provides you* with a realistic estimate of the value of your house, in both its present condition and once any needed repairs and updates are made, to help you see the value of those repairs and updates.

HOME BUYING EXPERIENCES

After having a bad experience with a representative of a home buyer company who breached the contract they had made with us, I was extremely grateful to find Ben. ... I didn't feel pressured or hassled as we had been with the other company. The closing was able to be done very quickly and it really was a seamless process. I was grateful not to have to deal with inspectors or to do staging and have multiple showings.

—Carol Moore

To this list of key value-adds, I would add one more: the agent should be a member of the *Home Downsizing Solutions Network* so that they can connect you with the excellent suite of services we've talked about through this book. These agents will begin at the beginning with you.

Figure out the best way to sell your house based on your particular situation. You want it just right. Getting it close to right only works in horseshoes and hand grenades—not real estate agents.

And getting it right for you may mean listing your house with a reputable realtor, or it may mean working with a realtor who also works with a home buying professional—to maximize the options you have on a very important sale.

Sometimes a home buyer is the best alternative

As an industry, home buying has also been flooded in recent years, with companies small and large moving into the home buying arena that I helped popularize twenty-five-plus years ago as a veteran just going into business and now today with *Home Downsizing Solutions*.

Among these new home buyers, often called iBuyers, there are big outfits that have tried to automate and scale up the practice of home buying. Real estate brokerages such as eXp Realty have built up a global operation with some 88,000 agents in local areas who work with home buying companies and make cash offers for houses in their area.

SENIOR DOWNSIZING EXPERIENCES

My sister owned an older home that she could no longer maintain. I helped her in finding and working with Ben ... every part of the process was explained clearly to us. He was upfront and honest and made my sister a very fair offer. The process was very quick and easy, my sister and I would like to thank Ben for his professionalism!!

—Bill Chapman

Big is not necessarily bad in home buying, though it is surely far less personalized. If there's a "bad" in many of these outfits, it's that their local operatives are looking for houses to buy on the cheap and dump into a portfolio of houses that a large private equity company will turn into an investment portfolio. That may work for the investors, but there is no concern for (a) the meaning the house has to the seller and (b) how the sale of the house fits into the next step in life. These are vital bits in a downsizing process done properly—respecting the homeowner as a fellow human being in the transaction.

TOP BBB RATING

After three other home buyers told me they couldn't help me and my situation was just too complicated, Ben took on and handled my difficult situation in a timely manner and with a wonderful outcome.

—Debra Sly (5 stars on Google)

These big home buying outfits also live and die on the property market cycle. When the market is rising they are rushing in; when the market again falls they close up shop. Many hundreds of these so-called home buyers went out of business in the housing collapse of 2008 and again to a lesser extent in 2020. Having a home buyer who knows the long-term ups and downs of the market—because they have kept the doors open through them—can be counted as a stable ally in the transition process.

My own company has purchased well over six hundred houses and helped several hundred more homeowners with a traditional sale of their house. We have done it one-on-one. When others have come along with automated systems to scale up their opportunities and profits, our team has continued to view each home purchase as a solution to provide for an individual in our community. We've been accused of being old-fashioned in that way. Fine!

In working with a senior looking to downsize, the first questions we ask are as follows:

☐ What are you hoping to accomplish?
☐ Is this the best time for you to be selling?
☐ If it is, should you use an agent, sell it yourself, or use a home buyer?

And often the next question is:

☐ Why would I want to sell my house to a home buyer?

This question can be answered many ways, as we've seen in this book. But to recap, it really comes down to your *agreeing* with most or all of these next six statements:

SPEED OF HOME BUYING

I met Ben and five days later I had a check in my pocket. Everyone was very courteous and responsive when I called ... I recommend them to anyone selling a home.

—James Spikula

☐ I don't want the hassle of listing the house.
☐ I don't want to do any repairs and updates or the cleaning to get the house market-ready.

☐ I don't want the hassle and stress of showings and strangers walking through the house whenever they want to.

☐ I don't want to handle inspections and appraisals and all the nit-picking buyers will do to negotiate down the price they already agreed to.

☐ I do want more certainty about when the sale will close and when I can move.

☐ I do want to know with certainty how much I will net from the sale.

If most of these six statements resonate with you, if you would enjoy downsizing far more with these four don'ts and two do's, then using a home buyer is going to give you a lot more peace of mind in the process while eliminating a lot of the stress and hassles that can come with a traditional sale.

And yet, you may not be convinced. I've talked with a lot of people who take it all in, take good notes, and still ask, "What's the catch?" The assumption is that there must be some hidden costs in selling a house in this manner.

There are no hidden costs, but there are variables that you want to take into account just as you would in working with an agent or selling it yourself. Let's look at those variables by first revisiting the handy chart from the last chapter.

House Selling Options

	REALTOR	FSBO	HOME BUYER
Commissions or Fees	6%	0	0
Closing Costs	Up to 8%	Up to 8%	0
Appraisal Required	Yes	Yes	No
Showings	Yes	Yes	No
Repairs/Renovations	Yes	Yes	No
Average Selling Time	60-90 Days	6-12 Months	3-21 Days

In selling a house with an agent, you will have a number of transaction costs: commissions paid to agent; discounts the buyer will ask for—especially in a flat or down market; closing costs, fees, and title insurance. These transaction costs can run up to 25 percent of the original asking price—so they are real and substantial costs.

If you use a home buyer instead, the initial offer you receive may, in fact, be lower than the price you would have listed at. But a home buyer in the *Home Downsizing Solutions Network* will pay all of the closing costs, so the offer price is a *net* price—the actual cash you receive, not a starting number that multiple items are subtracted from. So the difference between a listing price and a home buyer price can in the end be very small. More precisely.

In looking at all of the homes I've bought over twenty-five years, I've found that the net proceeds my sellers received averaged approximately 5–10 percent less than if they sold the house the traditional way. In return for this 5–10 percent difference, the sellers enjoyed a quick and stress-free sale along with help in transitioning to the next stage in life.

This "help" can manifest in many ways. For instance, some of my past clients have not wanted to take all the proceeds from the house sale in a lump sum. They either didn't need the funds right away or could get a better return on their money by taking a payment option and higher sale price for their house rather than just put the sale proceeds into the bank, or they wanted the funds kept away from certain members of the family. There have been a number of reasons.

But in this case, if the funds are not needed right away, I can step in as a home buyer and offer a much higher price for the house than if it was all-cash. We can structure a solution that pays out the cash you need at a later date or on a schedule that meets your needs.

This kind of custom solution is an example of how *Home Downsizing Solutions* can work for you individually, as a partner in a successful transaction.

"Are you a legitimate home buyer?"

As I noted, there are too many less-than-reputable outfits calling themselves home buyers that you should beware of. With new technologies at their disposal, there is no real barrier to entry anymore for folks who want to call themselves home buyers. They can easily throw up a website, run a bunch of online ads, and make themselves look legitimate.

Many of these companies, even those with nationwide footprints, have no intention of actually buying houses. They are actually wholesalers with good phone sales skills. Their reps spend their days calling their quota of 1,000 people in hopes of finding one or two they can talk into signing a binding agreement—whether the seller understands all the legal details or not.

Once these companies get an agreement to buy a house, they then go shopping for a buyer to sell the contract to, at a markup. And then they wait for that actual new homeowner to close on the sale before you ever get paid your lesser share. This process can take weeks and often months to conclude.

HOME BUYING EXPERIENCES

I've worked with [Ben] for over six years as the closing agent for Cornhusker Land Title in Omaha and have closed over two hundred transactions with them. What I have found that the sellers on our transactions have appreciated most, was the quick turnaround in closing, a typical sale happens in five or less days (unless there is an unforeseen title issue), also, that they are the actual purchaser of the property and do not assign the contract to another party. Because of these benefits I have worked with several happy sellers and will continue my support and referrals.

—Cheryl Royalty

One of the biggest problems with this is not hard to see. What if the wholesaler cannot find another buyer to take the contract? The wholesaler either backs out of the agreement, bringing in the lawyers to make it hard for the seller to object. Or the contract stretches out for many, many months, while the wholesaler looks for someone to "buy the contract" as they call it. Meanwhile, the seller is stuck in limbo unable to get on with life.

So, how do you find a trusted, legitimate home buyer?

"Are you going to look at my house?"

These home buying wholesalers all work pretty much the same way. Once you come to an agreement with them, they ask you to send them pictures of the house. They also look up your house on Zillow and the like, to get the basic details. Then they package the photos and details in an online advertisement—looking for a real buyer.

They'll tell you they need a twenty-one-day closing so that their inspectors have time to look over the house. Sounds fair enough. Except that these "inspectors" are actually potential buyers who are coming in to look at the house to see if they're interested in buying.

In this sense, you might as well use an agent because you're going to have people tromping through the house.

Then if an agreement is reached and there is a buyer, that buyer may well want to bring in their own inspector to make sure all systems are in order. If that inspection wasn't made earlier by the wholesaler (and it rarely is), then you can expect the offer they made to adjust downward as the new inspector (inevitably) finds some problem that (definitely) needs fixing.

Again, in this sense, you might just as well begin with an agent because you're not only going to have people tromping through the house, but the price will be renegotiated late in the game.

Some home buying companies even resort to the nastiest practice. They make you an offer that seems extremely good, higher than you expected, so you say yes. Only later, once they've inspected the house do they apologize and say that, whoops, they didn't realize the HVAC system is outdated, the foundation is cracked, the attic is overrun with mold, and on and on. They say these problems were not apparent in the photos (here they are being truthful—such problems don't show up in the house photos). So now, they're afraid, and the price will have to be lowered.

HOME BUYING EXPERIENCES

I'm currently on active duty and stationed in Washington DC. I'd been managing a house that my sister owned in Lincoln since the pandemic hit ... it quickly became too difficult for me to manage logistically. I contacted Ben, explained the situation, and [he] coordinated everything ... and offered us a fair price for the property. I do have a high preference for working with veterans and veteran-owned businesses, and Ben and the team ... are the perfect example of why.

—**Sean Spence**

All of these could have been avoided by using a home buying service that not only knows the local market and the nuances of home pricing in your area but also knows who is known locally as a reputable company.

Only one thing stops a legitimate home buying company from closing swiftly, and that's the title company's title check and closing paperwork preparation. This should happen in seven days or less, if all is in order with the title. And it will if the home buying company has a good relationship with a title and closing company in your area.

"How did you come up with the offer?"

When it comes to the offer you receive for your house, the home buying company should be able to explain how they arrived at it, whether you like the offer or not.

They should show you comparables and explain what they based their offer on.

They should have a worksheet that clearly shows the steps they took, and the calculations they made, to arrive at your offer.

At *Home Downsizing Solutions*, we have a Transaction Worksheet that we've used for years. It shows (a) the house's comparables in the area, (b) the house's current value as is, (c) what will be required to update the house to sell in "nice" condition, and (d) the transaction costs we will incur in buying, holding, and reselling the house. All the expenses we expect to incur will be laid out in the worksheet so that our clients have a transparent view on the process.

Selling a house is a major financial transaction, so we do all we can to thoroughly explain how we come up with our offers. Other companies should be able to explain as much to you, as well.

"Do you provide multiple offers or solutions?"

If a home buying company says that the only thing they can do is to buy your house (for a low cash price), they might not be the best option for you.

SENIOR EXPERIENCES

Ben was very patient and professional working with us as we helped my mom sell her house so that she could transition to assisted living. We ran into a snag with an old refi that the company had gone out of business but had not properly filed a lien release. Ben was willing to wait until we could get it resolved and kept his word on the original offer. He was prompt, professional and easy to work with even though I live out of state.

—Sharon Heaton (5 stars on BBB)

Just like if a real estate agent tells you the only thing they can do is to list your house, they might not be the best option for you.

That's why we review all the alternatives in selling a house and explain the positives and negatives in your particular situation. We also help you at each step of the downsizing process as you've seen here with *Home Downsizing Solutions*.

I want you to have the best. That's why I'm providing this concierge assistance as an extension of my own business. If you still have questions or I can help you in any way, don't hesitate to reach out.

- *Call our office*: 855-291-5005
- *Visit our website*: HomeDownsizingSolutions.com
- *Scan this QR code* with your phone and begin a text conversation with our team

Home Downsizing Solutions professionals are also available to give complimentary talks to senior communities, civic groups, and churches to help ensure more successful downsizings for our friends and neighbors in the years ahead.

15

The Home Downsizing Solutions Network Is Expanding

Interested in going to work on the most fulfilling side of real estate? Consider joining the *Home Downsizing Solutions Network* of professionals. You'll be helping seniors find the most stress-free way to sell their current house and move onto their next step in senior living. You'll work with house sellers who appreciate our uniquely professional home buying services.

No other network serves seniors like this

There are plenty of home buyers such as HomeVesters ("We buy ugly houses," boasting 1,200 locations). A few networks serve seniors looking into senior living. But no other network buys homes directly from seniors and helps them transition to the next stage—offering a genuinely caring solution to people at a time when it's truly valued.

We provide funding for the purchase

If you are in real estate now and want to expand your services to seniors, we provide the funding for home purchases for our network partners, so you have a twenty-five-plus year proven partner in your expanding business.

Leverage our deep experience

We've built a world-class support structure to enable our network partners to serve seniors with a proven business model, so there's no starting from scratch. You'll receive comprehensive training and ongoing support from initial training to ongoing coaching and assistance, marketing and operations support to reach potential customers, and build the *Home Downsizing Solutions Network* brand in your local market.

What makes the network so valuable?

As you must know, our nation's senior population is growing at an unprecedented pace and will continue to for decades to come. As seniors age, they turn their focus to downsizing and simplifying their lives. This means they are looking for new often-smaller homes and living community options.

These seniors are also a neglected segment of the market, certainly as far as senior transitions are concerned. So this is an opportunity to assist a segment of society that needs more help than it is receiving (exactly the opposite of younger real estate buyers and sellers who often get more help than they need). So you move into a win-win situation.

Benefits of a cash home sale for seniors

These are the big reasons seniors are welcoming the home buying alternative to the traditional listing approach:

- ☐ Ability to complete the deal in days, instead of many months.
- ☐ Ability to get a fair price that comes close to market price.
- ☐ No need to do home repairs, inspections, staging, or cleaning.
- ☐ No showings to strangers, nobody entering the house.
- ☐ Leave any or all of the "stuff."
- ☐ Homeowners can sell on their own timeline—as fast or slow as they need.
- ☐ No need for temporary financing to move into senior living.
- ☐ House can be sold, and the seller can stay in the house up to ninety days or longer if uncertain about when they can move into the senior living community.
- ☐ It's a one-stop solution for selling the house and downsizing—that works!

Want to learn more about the *Home Downsizing Solutions Network*? Contact Ben Souchek and ask about the support you'll receive in building a successful business. In the network, we're all stronger! Call our office: 855-291-5005.

Appendix

The senior community tour guide

Use this worksheet as a summary guide you can bring along on your tours of assisted living communities to help you evaluate and rank them by the criteria that matter most before making your choice.

LOOKING AROUND, WHAT DO YOU OBSERVE?

- ☐ Does the community feel "right sized" for your loved one?
- ☐ Are the hallways wide, elevators easily accessed, exits clearly marked?
- ☐ Is the staff keeping the place clean?
- ☐ Does it smell pleasant in all areas?
- ☐ Are the public rooms all free of clutter and tidy?
- ☐ Are the outdoor areas inviting and safe-looking?
- ☐ Are the residents interacting cheerfully with the staff?
- ☐ Do the residents look well groomed, with good hygiene?
- ☐ Are the rooms/apartments inviting, with good views?

☐ Will the decor uplift your loved one's mood each day?

☐ Are pets allowed, if your loved one wants to bring one?

WHAT IS THE COMMUNITY LIKE AT DIFFERENT TIMES OF DAY?

☐ When you swing by, are you greeted and feel welcome?

☐ In the morning, are the residents awake and well groomed?

☐ Around midday, are the residents up and engaged in activities?

☐ In the evening, are the residents interacting around the dinner table?

☐ Are the meals nutritious and appealing? (Join in a meal!)

☐ What do the residents themselves think about the community?

IS A PRIORITY PUT ON SAFETY AND SECURITY?

☐ Is the environment free of clutter or possible obstructions?

☐ Is there a system in place to handle emergencies?

☐ Is a licensed nurse on staff, and during what hours?

☐ Is there an easy-to-use emergency call system?

☐ Are there handrails in the hallways?

☐ Are there grab bars in the bathrooms and seats in the showers?

DO YOU UNDERSTAND ALL THE COSTS INVOLVED?

☐ What are the monthly fees?

☐ Do the fees cover room, board, and care for a particular level of assistance, or is there an à la carte charging method?

☐ What additional charges can or might be levied?

☐ Are there pricing incentives or other financial programs available?

☐ Is there a wait list, and how are available rooms allotted?

☐ What happens when a resident needs specialized care?

☐ Under what conditions would a resident be asked to move?

☐ Is the senior required to take a health assessment before moving in?

CAN THE COMMUNITY BE IDEAL FOR YEARS TO COME?

☐ Is the community ideal now and for the longer term, if that is the plan?

☐ If a move is necessary, how will the community help with this transition?

☐ No matter the reason for leaving, what type of notice will you have to give?

WHAT QUESTIONS ARE MOST IMPORTANT TO ASK?

☐ What types of living spaces are available?

☐ Are there individualized plans for residents?

☐ What type of security and safety measures are used?

☐ What kinds of medical services are available?

☐ Is there a nurse on duty at all times of the day?

☐ How are emergencies handled?

☐ How many staff members care for each resident?

☐ What type of training does the staff complete?

☐ Is transportation readily available?

☐ Is there a full activity and events calendar?

☐ What are the monthly fees and other possible expenses?

☐ Under what circumstances will residents have to move?

Moving into a senior community can become a delightful experience for everyone involved if good research is done and you're fully prepared. Hopefully this worksheet will help you choose a home that not only caters to you or your senior's needs but also suits personality and lifestyle desires.

 And if you need further help in this transition, that assistance is provided as a complimentary service by *Home Downsizing Solutions*. Our network of downsizing professionals can help at every step of the process, so please don't hesitate to contact us if we can help.

- *Call our office*: 855-291-5005
- *Visit our website*: HomeDownsizingSolutions.com
- *Scan this QR code* with your phone and begin a text conversation with our team

The home downsizing solutions six-month plan

This plan is designed to turn the drudgery of downsizing into a delight (almost!).

That's made possible by leaving you in control of the decision-making but having concierge services available to you as needed. It's the idea behind the hundreds of senior downsizing professionals I've brought together under the banner of *Home Downsizing Solutions*.

In working with these professionals, you'll want to follow this six-month plan. Hand off the tasks to them that you want to hand off; keep the rest for yourself to complete at *your* pace over six months, ideally. But let your own schedule dictate whether these six services take six months to complete, six weeks, or six days. So in we go.

1. BEGIN SLOW AND EASY—THE RIGHT WAY TO DOWNSIZE

☐ Before you begin, choose one room in the old house as a retreat room—a place of calm in the weeks ahead where you can pause and reflect on the memories and moments this house has given you and draw strength for the labors ahead.

☐ Retain a Senior Move Manager, if you'd like to, to help decide what you will be able to take with you and what you won't, help pack up everything for moving day, and then unpack in your new home.

☐ Make a list of all your belongings in the house—whether handwritten or on a spreadsheet.

☐ Take photos of everything so that you have a record and can use your old furniture layout to guide the layout in your new home, and plan ahead for adjustments based on the size of your new home.

☐ Take photos of all electronics from the rear view—to make sure all the wires and cords are restored to their proper locations.

☐ Make an inventory of valuables, and decide if anything should be appraised.

☐ Once you know the square footage of your new home, begin deciding what you will be able to bring along. You can then sell, donate, or dispose of those items (you're just starting, so some things are just to think about).

☐ Think about the major appliances—will you need to move them, or will they be handled in the new home or community?

☐ Will you need your car in your new neighborhood?

☐ Write out a budget and give it three parts. (This budget will help you manage the move and make decisions about which big items should come with you and which should be replaced in the new home. These figures will change, but they will help you plan and adjust as you go.)

    ▫ Current monthly expenses

    ▫ Expense after you move (to the extent you know them)

3. Onetime moving out costs (repairing the house for sale, moving company, moving insurance, equipment rentals, packing supplies)

2. YOUR STUFF WILL ALL FIND THE RIGHT HOME

☐ Create four piles in separate places in the house: to give away, to donate, to sell, to dump. Some people add a fifth pile: can't decide. (You can always come back to it!)

☐ Begin the sorting in the small spaces: outdoor sheds and garages, hall closets, linen closets, junk drawers, attics and crawl spaces, corners of the basement. It's easiest to begin here since this is where a lot of "junk" can accumulate. Throw out stuff you've long forgotten about.

☐ Make a first pass at your clothes and shoes, telling yourself that you'll get rid of items you haven't worn in (two, five, seven, ?) years.

- ☐ Move next into the kitchen. Purge the pantry of food items you won't be needing (or wait, and dump last minute). This room is full of items you use all the time. Don't think about what you have to get rid of; think about what you don't want to live without. Keep just those items.
- ☐ Collect all your cleaning products in one place. Try to use them up and not buy more before the move.
- ☐ Gather up all your important documents, and store them in a safe place. Do this with close family or a lawyer's help.
- ☐ Reduce your collection of books, DVDs, and CDs to a bare minimum.
- ☐ Gather up photo albums, recipe books, and other written items you may not have room for in your new home, and take them to a service to digitize them. Or do it yourself, since it's so easy now. You and your family will have a digital copy of your family's memories to hold on to.
- ☐ Eliminate duplicates. Cast off that second wool jacket, or that third serving dish, or a collection you may not have space for. Keep only the items you really need.
- ☐ Keep just your best artwork, photographs, and memorabilia to hold your memories close to your heart.
- ☐ If the possessions you can't or don't want to take to the new home are valued near to $10,000 or more, contact an estate sale or auction company to liquidate for you.
- ☐ It can be difficult to discard more valuable belongings. So ease the pain by donating any items you can to charities and people in need.
- ☐ Go to your four piles, and begin giving away, donating, selling, or dumping.
  - ☐ Hold a yard sale.

- ▫ Give items to charity.
- ▫ Place items in consignment or pawn shops.
- ▫ Try to sell them online.

3. YOUR HOUSE WILL BE READY TO SELL

Walk the house, going through every room, opening every closet and cabinet, laying fresh eyes on it all. Try to see it all for the first time (the way a potential buyer sees it). Ideally have an advisor with you. A realtor can be valuable, but a realtor wants only to sell the house fast—that may not be your best option. A Senior Move Manager can be helpful, because they are looking out for your interests. A *Home Downsizing Solutions* consultant can also bring insights and options for you to choose best.

You want the house to look spacious, clean, and well cared for.

You're going to be having strangers in your home; make sure you secure small valuables, firearms, and important papers. Remove any personal photos or items on display.

In your walk-through, you may find quite a few things that need to be done to the house to make it show-ready. At this point, you could bring in a home buying service to take your home as is, or you can begin updating and fixing up the house now.

- ☐ Paint the house.
- ☐ Install new floor coverings.
- ☐ Make cosmetic updates.
- ☐ Make the landscaping and garden stand out.
- ☐ Renovate the kitchen.
- ☐ Renovate the bathrooms.
- ☐ Fix or update major structural systems.

- ▫ Worn roof or cracks in the foundation are signs that expensive repairs may be needed. And a buyer may not qualify for a loan or insurance if these systems are not in good order.
- ▫ A roof needs to have several more years of life in it. The heating and cooling systems, as well as the plumbing, need to be in good working order. A home inspection will shine the light of discovery on these items.

Lastly, hire a moving company, and schedule a move date.

4. YOU'LL FIND YOUR BEST NEW HOME

Finalize the decision on your new home. Most likely you know where you're moving to. If you are moving into a smaller home, begin looking at homes in areas that interest you. Talk with real estate agents, and look at online listings, to get ideas. If you are moving into an assisted living community, begin looking at your options.

Prepare for your new space when you know more about it. Get a copy of the floor plans of the new home, or bring a tape measure and figure out dimensions and how your furniture will fit.

Start packing. You know which items you move with you because all else went into the four piles program. Mark every item that's going with you with a sticky note to direct the movers where to place the items in the new home.

5. MOVING OUT WILL GO SMOOTHLY FOR YOU

Now comes the big moving day! If you've been doing each step faithfully, this fifth should go smoothly. This is the time, working with your Senior Move Manager if you're choosing to, to finalize all of the preparations and check everything off as complete:

- ☐ All donations have been dropped off or picked up.
- ☐ An estate sale or auction is scheduled or done.
- ☐ Home repairs, upgrades, and polishes are handled.
- ☐ Food in kitchen, pantry, and freezer are drawn down.
- ☐ A junk removal company is scheduled to take any remaining items.

6. THE HOUSE WILL SELL SUCCESSFULLY

In this final step, you'll sell the house in the manner best suited to your needs. If you choose to list your house, your real estate agent will guide you through all the steps. If you choose instead to quickly sell without the stress and hassles of a listing, your home buying specialist will make the process go as smoothly as possible for you.

Home Downsizing Solutions is a complimentary service aimed at helping navigate the downsizing process with a one-stop solution, making it easier for everyone involved, even making it delightful (almost!).

We wish you the happiest of transitions. If you could use the concierge assistance we've talked about here, from how to begin downsizing the right way, on through to selling your old house successfully, contact us today!

Call our office: 855-291-5005

Visit our website: HomeDownsizingSolutions.com

Scan this QR code with your phone and begin a text conversation with our team

Endnotes

1   MaryAnne and Herb's story, like others in these pages, is a composite of the real downsizing situations Ben Souchek has encountered over the years.

2   "Home in retirement: more freedom, new choices," Merrill Lynch & AgeWave, 2016, https://agewave.com/wp-content/uploads/2016/07/2015-ML-AW-Home-in-Retirement_More-Freedom-New-Choices.pdf.

3   "The future of retirement," Merrill Lynch & AgeWave, 2013: https://www.agewave.com/TheFutureofRetirementStudiesandMediaCoverage.pdf.

4   Joe Verghese, Cuiling Wang, Xiaonan Xue, and Roee Holtzer, "Self-Reported Difficulty in Climbing Up or Down Stairs in Nondisabled Elderly," *Archives of Physical medicine and Rehabilitation* 89, no. 1 (January 2008): 100–104, https://www.ncbi.nlm.nih.gov/pmc/articles/PMC2671033.

5   Aging.com, "Fact sheet: falls. The biggest threat to senior health and safety," August 2023, https://www.aging.com/falls-fact-sheet.

6   Lily Katz, "Homebuyer competition drops to lowest level in over two years," Redfin News, July 20, 2022, https://www.redfin.com/news/real-estate-bidding-wars-june-2022/.

7   "Existing-home sales housing snapshot," National Association of Realtors, 2023, https://www.nar.realtor/infographics/existing-home-sales-housing-snapshot.

8   "Caregiving in the United States 2020," AARP & National Alliance for Caregiving, May 14, 2020, https://www.aarp.org/ppi/info-2020/caregiving-in-the-united-states.html.

9   Elizabeth Harrington and Bill McInturff, "Working while caring: a national survey of caregiver stress in the U.S. workforce," Rosalyn Carter Institute for Caregivers, 2021, https://www.rosalynncarter.org/wp-content/uploads/2021/09/210140-RCI-National-Surveys-Executive-Summary-Update-9.22.21.pdf.

10   Robyn Correll, "Senior caregivers: how much should you charge for your services?" Care, June 6, 2023, https://www.care.com/c/how-much-charge-as-senior-caregiver/.

and

"Private pay home care rates: understanding how much home care costs," Nurse Next Door, August 3, 2023, https://www.nursenext-door.com/blog/how-much-does-senior-home-care-cost/.

11   Scott Steinberg, "The average cost to move across the country: 8 ways to save money, rocket mortgage," March 31, 2023, https://www.rocketmortgage.com/learn/cost-to-move-across-the-country.

12   IBISWorld, "Estate liquidation services industry in the US – market research report," January 19, 2023, https://www.ibisworld.com/united-states/market-research-reports/estate-liquidation-services-industry/.

13 "How much does an estate sale cost?" EstateSales.NET, 2023, https://www.estatesales.net/help/how-much-does-an-estate-sale-cost.

14 Lisa Gerstner, "Money-smart ways to get rid of your stuff," Kiplinger, March 4, 2015, https://www.kiplinger.com/article/real-estate/t029-c000-s002-money-smart-ways-to-get-rid-of-your-stuff.html.

15 American Veterans Aid, "Aid & attendance benefit," https://www.americanveteransaid.com/landing/lp_2/NEW/aid_and_attendance_2.html.

16 True Tamplin, "Trustee fees," Finance Strategists, May 24, 2023, https://www.financestrategists.com/estate-planning-lawyer/trustee-fees.

17 A Merrill Lynch Retirement Study in partnership with Age Wave, "Home in retirement: more freedom, new choices," 2016, https://agewave.com/wp-content/uploads/2016/07/2015-ML-AW-Home-in-Retirement_More-Freedom-New-Choices.pdf.

18 This worksheet is condensed from a guide developed by the US Department of Health and Human Services' Agency for Healthcare Research and Quality, https://www.ahrq.gov.

19 https://en.wikipedia.org/wiki/Parliamentary_Ombudsman.

20 Kim Nguyen, "Strengthening the aging and disability networks: use of volunteers in long-term care Ombudsman programs," NORC at the University of Chicago, 2017, https://acl.gov/sites/default/files/programs/2020-10/NORC%20Research%20Brief_Use%20of%20Volunteers_508.pdf.

21 Julie Washington, "'A second pair of eyes:' how patient advocates, hospital ombudsmen help navigate health-care maze," cleveland.com, September 29, 2019, https://www.cleveland.com/healthfit/2019/09/

patient-advocates-hospital-ombudsmen-are-meant-to-ease-the-load-do-they.html.

22   Sharon Silow-Carroll, Jennifer N. Edwards, and Aimee Lashbrook, "Reducing hospital readmissions: lessons from top-performing hospitals," The Commonwealth Fund, April 6, 2011, https://www.commonwealthfund.org/publications/case-study/2011/apr/reducing-hospital-readmissions-lessons-top-performing-hospitals.

23   "How much care will you need?" LongTermCare.gov, February 18, 2020, https://acl.gov/ltc/basic-needs/how-much-care-will-you-need#.

24   "Medicaid eligibility: 2023 income, asset & care requirements for nursing homes & long-term care," American Council on Aging, January 18, 2023, https://www.medicaidplanningassistance.org/medicaid-eligibility/.

25   Wenliang Hou, Wei Sun, and Anthony Webb, "Why do people lapse their long-term care insurance?" Center for Retirement Research, Boston College, 2015, http://crr.bc.edu/wp-content/uploads/2015/09/IB_15-17.pdf.

26   "Aid & attendance benefit," American Veterans Aid, n.d., https://www.americanveteransaid.com/landing/lp_2/NEW/aid_and_attendance_2.html.

27   "Publication 503, Cat. No. 15004M, child and dependent care expenses," Department of the Treasury, December 22, 2022, https://www.irs.gov/pub/irs-pdf/p503.pdf.

28   Ibid.

29   "Retirement plans FAQs regarding hardship distributions," IRS, April 18, 2023, https://www.irs.gov/retirement-plans/retirement-plans-faqs-regarding-hardship-distributions.

30　Tobie Stanger, "11 Ways to afford the assisted living care you need," Consumer Reports, August 31, 2017, https://www.consumerreports.org/personal-finance/11-ways-to-afford-the-assisted-living-care-you-need/.

31　Ibid.

32　Jeff Hoyt, "Nursing home costs in 2023," SeniorLiving.org, August 18, 2023, https://www.seniorliving.org/nursing-homes/costs/.

33　Andrew Dehan, "Home renovation costs in 2023," Rocket Mortgage, May 1, 2023, https://www.rocketmortgage.com/learn/home-renovation-costs.

34　Brenda Richardson, "Share of homes bought with all cash hits the highest level since 2014," Forbes, December 21, 2022, https://www.forbes.com/sites/brendarichardson/2022/12/21/share-of-homes-bought-with-all-cash-hits-the-highest-level-since-2014.

35　"Housing inventory: median days on market in the United States," FRED Economic Data, https://fred.stlouisfed.org/series/MEDDAYONMARUS.

36　"Best-of-breed technology and automation for a truly digital mortgage," ICE Mortgage Technology, n.d., https://www.icemortgagetechnology.com.

37　"Monthly membership report," National Association of Realtors, August 2023, https://www.nar.realtor/membership/monthly-report.